Greenhouse Gardening For Total Beginners

Mikkely S. Hansen

All rights reserved. Copyright © 2023 Mikkely S. Hansen

COPYRIGHT © 2023 Mikkely S. Hansen

All rights reserved.

No part of this book must be reproduced, stored in a retrieval system, or shared by any means, electronic, mechanical, photocopying, recording, or otherwise, without written permission from the publisher.

Every precaution has been taken in the preparation of this book; still the publisher and author assume no responsibility for errors or omissions. Nor do they assume any liability for damages resulting from the use of the information contained herein.

Legal Notice:

This book is copyright protected and is only meant for your individual use. You are not allowed to amend, distribute, sell, use, quote or paraphrase any of its part without the written consent of the author or publisher.

Introduction

This is your comprehensive guide to embarking on a journey into the world of greenhouse gardening. This manual is designed to equip you with the knowledge and skills needed to make the most of your greenhouse and cultivate a thriving garden.

Before you even consider buying a greenhouse, we'll explore crucial factors and considerations to ensure you make an informed choice. Our buyer's guide provides valuable insights into selecting the right greenhouse for your needs. Additionally, we'll compare greenhouses with polytunnels, helping you decide which option suits you better.

Once you're set up, the guide dives into what you can grow in both polytunnels and greenhouses, offering a glimpse into the wide variety of plants you can nurture. Efficiently managing the temperature within your greenhouse is vital, and we'll delve into heating, cooling, and ventilation processes to create the ideal environment for your plants.

Understanding factors affecting heat loss is essential to optimize your greenhouse's performance. We'll also cover irrigation techniques to reduce plant stress and ensure consistent water and fertilizer delivery.

Special attention is given to the cultivation of specific plants like tomatoes, peppers, and tropical fruits within a greenhouse. You'll find a fruit and veg growing calendar to help you plan and maximize your harvests.

Insects can pose a threat to your greenhouse garden, and our guide includes an extensive section on greenhouse insect management. Learn about common greenhouse insects and effective pest management strategies to protect your plants.

Finally, we emphasize the importance of cleaning your greenhouse and provide insights into ongoing maintenance practices to keep your greenhouse in top shape.

This book is your one-stop resource for all things related to greenhouse gardening. Whether you're a novice or an experienced gardener, this guide will empower you to create and maintain a flourishing greenhouse garden. Happy gardening!

Contents

WHAT TO CONSIDER BEFORE BUYING AGREENHOUSE 1
GREENHOUSE BUYER'S GUIDE 6
GREENHOUSE VS. POLYTUNNEL WHICH ONEIS BETTER? 12
WHAT CAN YOU GROW IN A POLYTUNNELAND A GREENHOUSE? 16
HOW TO EFFICIENTLY HEAT AND COOL AGREENHOUSE 25
GREENHOUSE HEATING, COOLING ANDVENTILATION PROCESS 29
FACTORS AFFECTING HEAT LOSS 34
HOW TO IRRIGATE YOUR GREENHOUSE TO REDUCES THE AMOUNT OF PLANT LOSS CAUSED BY STRESS ...... INDUCED BY DELIVERING AN INCONSISTENT AMOUNT OFWATER OR FERTILIZER 59
HOW TO GROW TOMATOES, PEPPER ANDTROPICAL FRUITS IN A GREENHOUSE   68
FRUIT AND VEG GROWING CALENDAR 86
GREENHOUSE INSECT MANAGEMENT 94
COMMON GREENHOUSE INSECTS ANDRELATED PESTS 95
GENERAL STRATEGIES FOR INSECT ANDMITE MANAGEMENT 116
WHY CLEAN YOUR GREENHOUSE? 123
Ongoing Greenhouse Cleaning andMaintenance 125
CONCLUSION 127

WHAT TO CONSIDER BEFORE BUYING A GREENHOUSE

With winter on its way, some gardeners are calling it quits and parting with their plants for the year. Others realize that the joys of gardening need not cease at the end of October. By buying a greenhouse, you can enjoy warm-weather flowers, fruits, and vegetables all year long.

You can buy your greenhouse at a local garden center, a hardware store, or online. Prices vary from anywhere between $300 for a basic setup to several thousand for more large-scale structures. But before you go shopping around for the better bargain, you need to determine what type of greenhouse is right for you. Your decision will depend on several factors.

1. External Climate

The climate where you live impacts the temperature inside your greenhouse. In general, a freestanding structure will allow you more control over greenhouse temperatures because it will be exposed to more regular sunlight than an attached greenhouse, which will be frequently shaded by your house, depending on the time of day.

2. Internal Climate

What temperature would you like to maintain inside your greenhouse? This factor won't affect what

greenhouse structure you'll need, but you may have to purchase some extra hardware to maintain your desired temperature. Greenhouse heaters can be powered by gas, propane, or electricity. Depending on the climate, you may only need to run the heater overnight.

If you just plan on starting or housing seedlings through the winter, a "cool greenhouse" that stays around 45 degrees Fahrenheit should be sufficient. You can protect your plants from winter frosts by covering your greenhouse with bubble insulation, available at most hardware stores. Some gardeners say a swimming pool solar cover works just as well.

You may need to up the temperature if you want to grow tender perennials, most of which will do well in a "warm greenhouse" with temperatures around 55 degrees Fahrenheit. To do this, you'll need to buy a greenhouse heater.

If you plan to grow tropical plants, which require temperatures of at least 65 degrees Fahrenheit, you'll need to run a more powerful heater, possibly day and night depending on the weather in your area. This type of greenhouse, known as a "hothouse", is the most expensive to maintain.

3. Stability

Another thing you should consider before running out to the store is whether you want a portable greenhouse or a permanent one.

If you live in an area with severe temperatures and lots of wind, you may want to take down your greenhouse and store it during unfavorable weather periods. On the other hand, some permanent greenhouses with foundations, while more expensive, may be sturdy enough to withstand harsh weather conditions.

4. Cost

A freestanding greenhouse may require a larger investment in electricity and heating since it stands apart from the rest of the house. Despite fluctuating temperatures, an attached greenhouse may lower your electric bill, since the heat generated inside the structure will help to warm your house. Plus, attached greenhouses carry the added benefit of convenience: simply step out the back door of your house, and you're in your garden paradise.

5. Permits

Evaluate your gardening needs to determine which type of greenhouse is right for you. Once you've decided, there's one last thing you need to do. Before you go out and buy your dream greenhouse, call your local building department and find out if you need a permit to build one in your area. In most towns, hobby greenhouses don't require a permit,

but it's a good idea to find out before you go out and buy yours. The last thing you want is to spend a bunch of time and money on your greenhouse only to get a call from a local official ordering you to take it down.

GREENHOUSE BUYER'S GUIDE

Gardeners view green houses as a dream or a necessity, the latter by those who already have them, the former by those who wish they did. A greenhouse serves many functions and grants many advantages. It's a place to give seedlings a jump start ahead of the growing season, a place to raise plants, including everything from tomatoes to lemons, that won't find the growing season they require outdoors. It's a place to overwinter potted plants and extend the vegetable harvest well past the first (and second, and third) frost. A green house can add immensely to your enjoyment of gardening and its rewards.

Specialized kits make owning a greenhouse easy. But what's the right setup for you? It's important to consider what you intend to do in your green house and then make sure you have the room and features those intentions require. If you're just planning to start some seedling for transplant or to harden off some starts before they're transplanted in the garden, you might consider a cold frame. But if your intent is to utilize your green house for any of the other uses above or a combination of multiple uses a green house is your best and most efficient option.

"The best way to keep plants protected from freezing temps!" Wall O Water Season Extenders sold in packs of 3 enable gardeners to start tomatoes, peppers, squash or other plants 6-8 weeks earlier, without fear of freezing. Protects down to 16°F.

Once you've decided what you'll be doing in your green house, consider how much space you'll need. Make sure you'll have the room inside the house for all you intend to do. Draw a to-scale floor plan of your greenhouse space using graph paper and find a place for potting benches, grow shelves, and places for large permanent residents, whether in pots or directly in the ground. Then add on a few more square feet.Out growing a green house after only a season or two is a common story among gardeners. Starting with a little more room than you think you'll need allows for your ambition to grow. More room most often pays for itself.

The next considerations concern which materials are best for your greenhouse's frame and glazing.It's important to consider weight and durability of the materials for each and which are best suited to your climate conditions and needs.

Do you want something lightweight that you can move to places in your garden where you want to extend the growing season, spring or fall? Do you need a glazing capable of withstanding the possibility of hail storms or resistant to deterioration from sunlight? Should the glazing be designed to insulate and conserve the cold-season heat generated by the sun? Will your frame be required to support winter snow loads without bending or collapsing?

Here are some tips to guide you in choosing both frames and glazing.

Frame Materials

• Wood is often the choice of do-it-yourselfers because of its availability and the ease with which it can be worked. Wood is also strong enough to support what ever glazing you might choose. Overtime, wood, unlike steel, aluminum or plastic, can be susceptible to rot. But with yearly attention and good drainage, wood can last a lifetime. Wood frames are heavy, providing good anchorage. Once assembled, a wood frame also allows for hooks and other attachments for shelves and hanging baskets. Many gardeners think wood is the most aesthetically pleasing of green house frame materials.

• Aluminum frames are durable, rust-proof, and relatively light weight. The pieces are often grooved or channeled to allow for easy placement of the glazing. They're an especially good choice for a first green house. Considerations: Aluminum frames conduct heat. They'll be hotter in the summer and give up warmth more quickly in the winter. Because of their light weight, some aluminum frame green houses are attached to a steel frame at ground level.

• Plastic framing is a good, inexpensive, and lightweight choice that's best for small green houses. It's often covered in types of plastic film that diffuse light effectively inside. Plastic frames do not conduct as much heat as metal frames. Because of their light-weight, they're often anchored on a steel frame. Inside tray supports and hanging racks are often steel-reinforced to increase the weight they can support.

• Steel is the heaviest of green house frame materials and is most frequently used for large, permanent, commercial structures. Because of its weight and difficulty to work with (including setting glazing), steel frames can be difficult to maintain.

Glazing

- Glass has aesthetic as well as historical appeal as a green house glazing. Tempered glass has taken a big bite out of the breakage problem, but glass is still heavy and expensive to replace. Un-tempered glass will eventually show wear and discoloring. Tempered glass will not. The thicker the glass green house glazing is often 3 or 4 millimeter thick– the more damage resistant it becomes. Still, winter storms and freezes can take their toll with breaks and cracks of tempered glass as well. Glass, unless treated or covered with special film, does not diffuse light to the plants beneath it.

- Polycarbonate frequently replaces glass in small back yard green houses. Despite its lightness, it's strong and durable. Polycarbonate panels are translucent, not transparent. letting in the kind of soft, diffused light that is most effective in green houses. They come in double and even triple-walled types to increase heat retention. Triple-walled polycarbonate makes for better insulated green houses but doesn't allow as much light in as double-walled types.

- Polyethylene sheeting is the least expensive glazing for green houses. It works well for small backyard greenhouses constructed of plastic frames. It's also used to cover large and long, steel-framed commercial green houses used to grow tomatoes, corn, cucumbers, and other heat-loving vegetables that need plenty of room. Polyethylene is particularly subject to fading and yellowing and even under the best conditions must be replaced in three to five years. It's also subject to tearing due to stretching caused by temperature extremes, winds, and snow loads. Among the three glazings listed, polyethylene allows the least amount of usable light into the green house.

Many of the so-called "accessories" that green house kits come with are crucial to the success of your inside gardening. Venting hot air up and out of the green house can mean the difference between vigorous, sun-drenched plants and wilted, heat-struck plants that probably won't survive the temperatures. How large a door will you need? Does it need to be wide enough to accept your garden cart? Will your growing shelves be freestanding or will they need support from the frame? Will you need a fan to move air in the winter to prevent freezing and when it's hot to pull it outside? Will you need a heater?

Again, these things depend on your needs and conditions. Making wise choices will be rewarded with wonderful growing.

GREENHOUSE VS. POLYTUNNEL WHICH ONE IS BETTER?

Site Preparation and Construction first:

Polytunnels can be constructed on a slightly uneven surface in a day. Greenhouses take longer to install. They should be also erected on a perfectly flat and levelled surface. There are several ways to prepare the ground for your greenhouse:

• Paving slabs base - They allow you to plant crops and flowers only into pots.

• Compacted soil base -You can plant your crops directly into the ground.

• Compacted soil and paving slabs base – It allows you to plant both in the soil and in containers.

People consider paving slabs to be the best base for a greenhouse. It helps prevent damp build-up and fungal problems, as well as diseases that uncovered soil can develop. Both types of structures should face North-South to avoid direct sunlight.

Ventilation:

Most of the plants may dry out if a change in temperature occurs.Polytunnels offer a much better control over its air circulation.Large doors at both ends provide sufficient air flow through the tunnel.Greenhouses provide ventilation through an opening on the roof, the door and side vents.Keep all doors and vents open during sunny days to achieve effective ventilation.

Durability:

When it comes to longevity, there isn't much of a difference between greenhouses and polytunnels. Both types can last for many years. Polytunnels can last between 15-20 years but the covers need to be replaced every few years. A common question asked is "How long does a polytunnel cover last?". Well, this will depend on where you've positioned the polytunnel structure. The plastic covers need a little care, too so you can ensure that they stay in good condition for a few years. Place your polytunnel on a spot, protected from strong winds.Clean the covers regularly from fallen leaves and trim nearby foliage. This will keep your polytunnels in good condition for longer.

Most greenhouses may even last for a lifetime if they are well taken care of. We have several tips on how to maintain a greenhouse:

• Scrub the windows to let more sunlight in.

• Frequently check and maintain the heating system components.

• Clean the floors and tables regularly.

• Let ladybugs and spiders in to control pests.

Which one is better looking:

Greenhouses can be the highlight of any garden, especially if they have a fancy design. They come in various shapes and models that you can choose from. Orangeries, Dwarf Wall or Victorian Style greenhouses are the most popular designs on the market.

Polytunnels, however, are a far more practical option but not so appealing. They can also come in various shapes, forms and sizes each of them with their own benefits. For instance, semi-circular arc-shaped polytunnels allow the rain to run easily off the surface. High-tent polytunnels, on the other hand, allow taller plants, such as tomatoes, to grow as high as they need.

Heat Retention and Shading:

These constructions protect crops from bad weather conditions. They create a pleasant environment by retaining heat and moisture. The plastic sheeting that polytunnels use also affects heat retention. Note that green polytunnel covers do not let enough light permeate through the tunnel. This makes transparent covers a much better option. Condensation issues in polytunnels can be resolved by installing Thermal Anti-Fog covers, which effectively reduce moisture levels. This type of sheeting can also improve heat retention.

Greenhouses offer maximum heat retention and better light transmission. But they are vulnerable to overheating, which is why plants need more shading. There are several ways to achieve that. Some people paint some of the glass panels to reduce the quantity of light coming through the structure. Fitting partially your greenhouse with external blinds will also have a similar cooling effect. The fixtures effectively prevent the sun's rays from passing through the glass. Internal blinds, on the other hand, stimulate heat generation as the sun passes through the glass.

Furthermore, it is important to make the right choice, regarding the type of glass you want to use for glazing your greenhouse. Buying toughened glass is a safer option because it breaks into blunt cubes. It is a bit more expensive than regular glass. In contrast, polycarbonate provides better insulation but it is likely to blow out of the frame in strong wind.

Internal Microclimate:

Specialised equipment controls the temperature, humidity, air flow and irrigation systems. Polytunnels are prone to drought and so are greenhouses. You might need to add an extra layer of bubble insulation to protect your plants better in cold weather.

The benefits of rainwater collection

Water collection is an important factor to keep in mind. Rainwater harvesting has many benefits. It is an eco-friendly process, a money saver and a nutrients supplier. Greenhouses are easier to adapt than polytunnels, with regards to fitting them with an effective rainwater harvest system. Well, a good solution to the water collection problem in polytunnels is using a gutter system. You can install a rainwater gutter to one of the sides of your polytunnel, leading straight into a water tank. This way, you'll have sufficient quantity of irrigation water that you can use whenever you need to.

WHAT CAN YOU GROW IN A POLYTUNNEL AND A GREENHOUSE?

What to grow in a polytunnel:

Fruits:

- Strawberries – Mix in some compost with the soil before you plant them.

- Raspberries – Add mulch to the soil to keep it moisturised.

- Melons – They like humid conditions and fertilised soil.

Vegetables:

- Tomatoes – Boost the soil by adding organic matter to it before planting.

- Cucumbers – Create vertical structure in order to allow the crops to grow.

- Artichokes – They thrive well thanks to the warmth and humidity that polytunnels create.

Herbs:

- Rosemary – It grows well in warm conditions and does not need frequent watering.

- Oregano – It helps soil moisture retention.

- Basil, Thyme, Chives – They repel various pests and protect the crops around them.

Trees:

• Peach – Polytunnels protect them from frost and birds that like their fruits.

• Apricot – They need some extra heating.

• Citrus (Lemon, Orange, Lime, Grapefruit) – Polytunnels retain the ideal temperature for them to thrive in the winter months.

Flowers:

• Tulips, Sweet Peas, Foxgloves, Lupins – They attract bees, pollinators and other beneficial insects.

What to grow in a greenhouse:

Flowers:

• Roses – They need enough moisture and around 6 hours of direct sunlight per day.

• Tulips – These plants need protection against pests and frost, so this is the perfect environment for them.

• Orchids – Provide them with the right temperature. Avoid over-watering them.

• Lupin – Constant sunlight and moisturised soil is what they need. Lupins can grow in most soils, even those that are poor in nutrients, except in chalky soil.

Vegetables:

- French Beans – A sunny spot and moisture is all they need.

- Aubergines – Warm the soil a couple of weeks before planting to protect them against frost.

- Peppers – Water and fertilise them regularly. Place peppers in a sheltered, sunny spot.

Fruits:

- Grapes – Water them frequently during the growing period.

- Kiwi Fruits – They should be grown in sheltered sunny spots.

Crop options are limitless. Both types of facilities create appropriate conditions for crop growing. Polytunnels are usually used for growing large amounts of fruits and vegetables. On the other hand, greenhouses are better-looking structures. They are often used for growing various classic or exotic flowers or even tropical fruit.

Advantages And Disadvantages

Advantages of Polytunnels:

- Polytunnels are a budget-friendly option.

- They can offer more growing space.

- Polytunnels are more flexible structures.

- They can be modified to incorporate various additional features or to achieve a specific purpose, such as widening the doors or expanding the plant beds.

- There is a possibility to increase the interior space.

Disadvantages of Polytunnels:

- They can be blown away by strong winds, which is why the frame should be attached to the ground properly.

- Polytunnels are prone to damage, caused by pets and birds.

- If the sheeting is not straight and tightened properly, condensation can build up and harm the plants, as high humidity levels promote mould growth.

- Covers need to be replaced every 5 years.

- They are harder to fit with a rainwater collection system.

Pros of a Greenhouse:

- Greenhouses are more visually appealing constructions.

- They are mainly used for growing flowers but you can grow crops in them as well.

- Most frames are made from powder coated aluminium, which protects them from oxidising.

- They protect plants better against pests.

- If you use toughened glass, they can withstand bad weather conditions, too.

Cons of a Greenhouse:

• Site preparation requires a lot of effort. The base must be firm and flat.

• It can take up to several months to get your custom-made greenhouse delivered to you. Unless you want to buy a standard-size one.

• Greenhouses are more complex structures. It takes professionals a couple of days to install one.

• They are expensive and difficult to move as well.

• If damaged, you're likely to be looking at replacing several glass panels.

• Since most people prefer to position their greenhouse next to the house, there isn't always enough space to install it.

• Apart from the construction itself, supplying kits and electric heaters are not cheap, either.

Before you make a decision, take your time to plan and define your needs. Both structures come in various shapes and sizes. Greenhouses are appropriate for you if you want something extra appealing for your garden. They create optimal environment for various exotic plants. On the other hand, polytunnels are something you might not want to place next to your house but in the backyard instead. Being easily expandable makes them appropriate for growing large quantities of edible plants and start up various flowers from seeds. They are more flexible and are the less expensive option, too.

Did You Know Why Are Greenhouses Called 'Green'?

Greenhouses are eco-friendly structures which reduce energy bills. They are also good for the environment. They improve the air around your house.

A common question asked is 'Why are greenhouses called green when they are invariably clear glass or plastic'. According to some studies, greenhouses are called this way because they used to be treated with a green dye. It absorbed light and produced heat. In fact, people still use it today in salt production. It increases the absorption of UV lights by the sea in order to speed up evaporation.

Greenhouse sheeting is usually made from translucent materials clear plastic or glass. This allows sunlight to come in and stimulate the photosynthesis process. It combines carbon dioxide and sunlight's energy which feed the plants. Around 6 hours of daily sunlight exposure is what plants need thoroughly.

Greenhouse Foundation Options

In colder climates or wherever you want to grow vegetables and plants when the weather is not ideal, a greenhouse is the way to do it, but in order to support it you will need to build a greenhouse foundation. A greenhouse consists of a metal frame with either glass or composite panes. Although not nearly the weight of a garage let alone a house, a greenhouse nonetheless needs a good support system to stay level and workable. There are a number of different materials you can use to build your greenhouse foundation.

Concrete, brick and timber are the three that will be discussed here, briefly outlining the pros and cons of each.

Concrete

Laying a concrete foundation for your greenhouse will be the most durable option. A concrete foundation benefits from its inherent strength and uniformity. Properly framed, a foundation made from concrete will last a long time, and if it is correctly sealed, it will be protected from the elements. For large greenhouses, a concrete foundation makes the most sense as the greater the weight of the frame, the more important it is to have a solid structure supporting it.

On the other hand, pouring a slab of concrete large and thick enough to support a greenhouse can be both time consuming and expensive.If you were to hire a contractor, it could easily run into the thousands of dollars. Doing it yourself may save you some money, but the labor involved is extensive.

Brick

Another option for a greenhouse foundation is brick. With a properly smoothed and leveled bed of earth, interlocking brick pavers can be laid that offer support for a greenhouse comparable to concrete. Although labor intensive, it is less so than pouring your own concrete foundation. And unlike concrete, if ever a section of brick were to crack, replacement is a matter of changing out the necessary number of bricks.

You can opt to simply fit the bricks together in an interlocking pattern or use mortar to secure them. Using mortar will require more labor and cost, but it will give you an even firmer base upon which to build a greenhouse. The initial cost of brick may exceed the raw materials required for pouring a concrete foundation, but there is a mutual tradeoff of labor vs. cost between the two options.

Timber

A timber foundation, or one constructed out of lumber, is yet another option. For homes, garages and other buildings, the lowest level of lumber is always secured to a concrete foundation. Thus, merely laying out a few slabs of wood for a foundation will work only for the smallest of greenhouses. If the land is very flat and level and the greenhouse is of modest size, constructing a foundational frame out of pressure treated wood is a viable option. Use 4 to 6 concrete support blocks with brackets built in. These in turn support 4x6 floor beams which support the appropriate number of 2x6 floor joists. Atop these go plywood or another type of sub floor, followed by any linoleum or flooring of your choice. If your greenhouse is not too big, this is a very workable idea that won't cost you as much as hiring a concrete crew or purchasing hundreds of interlocking bricks.

Several different materials are available to you for your greenhouse foundation. Concrete, brick and lumber all present an effective way to support a greenhouse, whatever its size. Cost, labor and strength are all factors to consider before you make a choice.

HOW TO EFFICIENTLY HEAT AND COOL A GREENHOUSE

When installing a heating system to your greenhouse, you must follow some basic requirements. Keep in mind that a greenhouse is only as efficient as its heating system after all, providing a warm environment to your plants is the whole purpose of a greenhouse! When planning an efficient greenhouse heating system, everything has to be properly sized to cater to extreme temperatures and, for the sake of your pocketbook and the planet, carefully planned to avoid heat loss. Here's some basic steps to take to when it comes to creating an effective heating system for your greenhouse.

Get Accurate Dimensions of the Greenhouse Itself

Knowing the correct length, width, and height of your greenhouse is fundamental to installing the proper heating system to ensure that it will always provide the correct temperature without over- or under-heating. This is necessary to provide your plants with the correct environment to support growth. Make sure you go through the process of measuring the greenhouse more than once to get accurate numbers.

Install Insulation to Keep the Heat from Escaping the Greenhouse

Your greenhouse's heat loss will be amplified if you fail to include insulation measures in the structure. Insulation is available in a variety of forms and can be as simple as night shades or a polyethylene liner, or a more complex double glazing of the glass. While double glazing is efficient, it is a more costly option. For a more budget-friendly alternative, you can install bubble sheets instead. While they will have to be replaced every few years, bubble sheets are very efficient in reducing heat loss. (If your greenhouse shares a heated wall in your house, that will also provide insulation.) Be aware that some types of insulation can cut off light, so install nothing that is permanently fixed.

Choose the Right Greenhouse Heating System

Once you have accurate calculations, you have to choose the right heating system for your greenhouse requirements. Some greenhouses are sold with a heating system included, but if you have a greenhouse that requires a separate heating system, there are several options. The first are electric-powered fan heaters, which are easy to use and won't cause pollution. These fan heaters blow hot air evenly and continuously around the greenhouse without leaving harmful damp spots within the structure. Another greenhouse heating option is a tubular heating unit that emits a soft, radiant heat. Instead of heating the air within the greenhouse, these units heat the soil and can be wired together to work in a parallel arrangement to produce more heat. A third option for a greenhouse heating source are propane gas heaters, which are very heat-efficient, relatively cheap to buy and install, and suitable for larger greenhouses as they produce more than enough heat. An even cheaper option uses kerosene as fuel. While a kerosene heater is the least expensive to run and produces a good amount of heat, kerosene has a distinct odor and causes atmospheric dampness, which could harm your plants. Kerosene heaters also need frequent and constant cleaning to work efficiently.

Isolate Plants that Require High Temperatures

Another efficient way to reduce heat loss in your greenhouse is to section off within the structure areas housing plants that specifically require high temperatures. You can then plan your heating system for that area of the greenhouse only, which will greatly reduce your heating requirements overall and keep your plants as healthy as possible in their own separate ecosystems.

Install an Alarm System in the Greenhouse that's Sensitive to Temperature

If your budget can cover it, you can also install an alarm system which will warn you if the temperature within the greenhouse should decrease unexpectedly. This alerts you to take action in regulating the termperature of the greenhouse, as well as safeguards your plants from sudden cold shock.

GREENHOUSE HEATING, COOLING AND VENTILATION PROCESS

Greenhouses should provide a controlled environment for plant production with sufficient sunlight, temperature and humidity. Greenhouses need exposure to maximum light, particularly in the morning hours. Consider the location of existing trees and buildings when choosing your greenhouse site. Water, fuel and electricity make environmental controls possible that are essential for favorable results. For this reason, use reliable heating, cooling and ventilation. Warning devices might be desirable for use in case of power failure or in case of extreme temperatures.

The house temperature requirements depend upon which plants are to be grown. Most plants require day temperatures of 70 to 80 degrees F, with night temperatures somewhat lower. Relative humidity may also require some control, depending on the plants cultured.

Some plants grow best in cool greenhouses with night temperatures of 50 degrees F after they are transplanted from the seeding tray. These plants include azalea, daisy, carnation, aster, beet, calendula, camellia, carrot, cineraria, cyclamen, cymbidium orchid, lettuce, pansy, parsley, primrose, radish, snapdragon, sweet pea and many bedding plants.

Some plants grow best in warm greenhouses with night temperatures of 65 degrees F. These plants include rose, tomato, poinsettia, lily, hyacinth, cattleya orchid, gloxinia, geranium, gardenia, daffodil, chrysanthemum, coleus, Christmas cactus, calla, caladium, begonia, African violet, amaryllis and tulip.

Tropical plants usually grow best in high humidity with night temperatures of 70 degrees F.

Heating

Georgia greenhouses must be heated for year-round crop production. A good heating system is one of the most important steps to successful plant production. Any heating system that provides uniform temperature control without releasing material harmful to the plants is acceptable. Suitable energy sources include natural gas, LP gas, fuel oil, wood and electricity. The cost and availability of these sources will vary somewhat from one area to another. Convenience, investment and operating costs are all further considerations.Savings in labor could justify a more expensive heating system with automatic controls.

Greenhouse heater requirements depend upon the amount of heat loss from the structure. Heat loss from a greenhouse usually occurs by all three modes of heat transfer: conduction, convection and radiation. Usually many types of heat exchange occur simultaneously. The heat demand for a greenhouse is normally calculated by combining all three losses as a coefficient in a heat loss equation.

Conduction

Heat is conducted either through a substance or between objects by direct physical contact. The rate of conduction between two objects depends on the area, path length, temperature difference and physical properties of the substance(s) (such as density). Heat transfer by conduction is most easily reduced by replacing a material that conducts heat rapidly with a poor thermal conductor (insulator) or by placing an insulator in the heat flow path. An example of this would be replacing the metal handle of a kitchen pan with a wooden handle or insulating the metal handle by covering it with wood. Air is a very poor heat conductor and therefore a good heat insulator.

Convection

Convection heat transfer is the physical movement of a warm gas or liquid to a colder location. Heat losses by convection inside the greenhouse occur through ventilation and infiltration (fans and air leaks).

Heat transfer by convection includes not only the movement of air but also the movement of water vapor. When water in the greenhouse evaporates, it absorbs energy. When water vapor condenses back to a liquid, it releases energy. So when water vapor condenses on the surface of an object, it releases energy to the outside environment.

Radiation

Radiation heat transfer occurs between two bodies without direct contact or the need for a medium such as air. Like light, heat radiation follows a straight line and is either reflected, transmitted or absorbed upon striking an object. Radiant energy must be absorbed to be converted to heat.

All objects release heat in all directions in the form of radiant energy. The rate of radiation heat transfer varies with the area of an object, and temperature and surface characteristics of the two bodies involved.

Radiant heat losses from an object can be reduced by surrounding the object with a highly reflective, opaque barrier. Such a barrier (1) reflects the radiant energy back to its source, (2) absorbs very little radiation so it does not heat up and re-radiate energy to outside objects, and (3) prevents objects from "seeing" each other, a necessary element for radiant energy exchange to occur.

FACTORS AFFECTING HEAT LOSS

Heat loss by air infiltration depends on the age, condition and type of greenhouse. Older greenhouses or those in poor condition generally have cracks around doors or holes in covering material through which large amounts of cold air may enter. Greenhouses covered with large sheets of glazing materials, large sheets of fiberglass, or a single or double layer of rigid or flexible plastic have less infiltration (Figure 1).

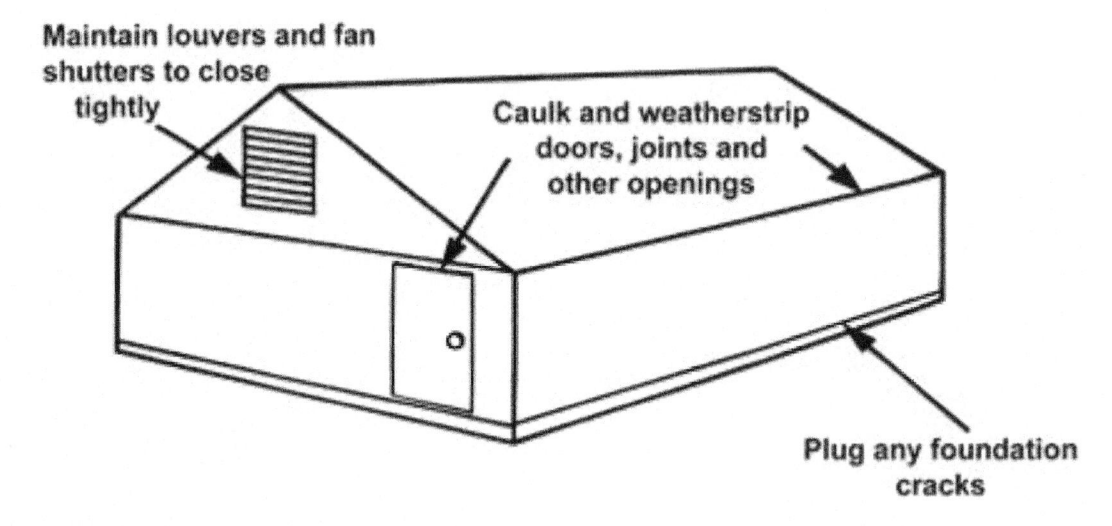

Figure 1. Energy loss due to infiltration.

The greenhouse ventilation system also has a large effect on infiltration. Inlet and outlet fan shutters often allow a large air exchange if they do not close tightly due to poor design, dirt, damage or lack of lubrication. Window vents seal better than inlet shutters, but even they require maintenance to ensure a tight seal when closed.

Solar radiation enters a greenhouse and is absorbed by plants, soil and greenhouse fixtures. The warm objects then re-radiate this energy outward. The amount of radiant heat loss depends on the type of glazing, ambient temperature and amount of cloud cover. Rigid plastic and glass materials exhibit the "greenhouse effect" because they allow less than 4 percent of the thermal radiation to pass back through to the outside.

The greenhouse ventilation system also has a large effect on infiltration. Inlet and outlet fan shutters often allow a large air exchange if they do not close tightly due to poor design, dirt, damage or lack of lubrication. Window vents seal better than inlet shutters, but even they require maintenance to ensure a tight seal when closed.

Solar radiation enters a greenhouse and is absorbed by plants, soil and greenhouse fixtures. The warm objects then re-radiate this energy outward. The amount of radiant heat loss depends on the type of glazing, ambient temperature and amount of cloud cover. Rigid plastic and glass materials exhibit the "greenhouse effect" because they allow less than 4 percent of the thermal radiation to pass back through to the outside.

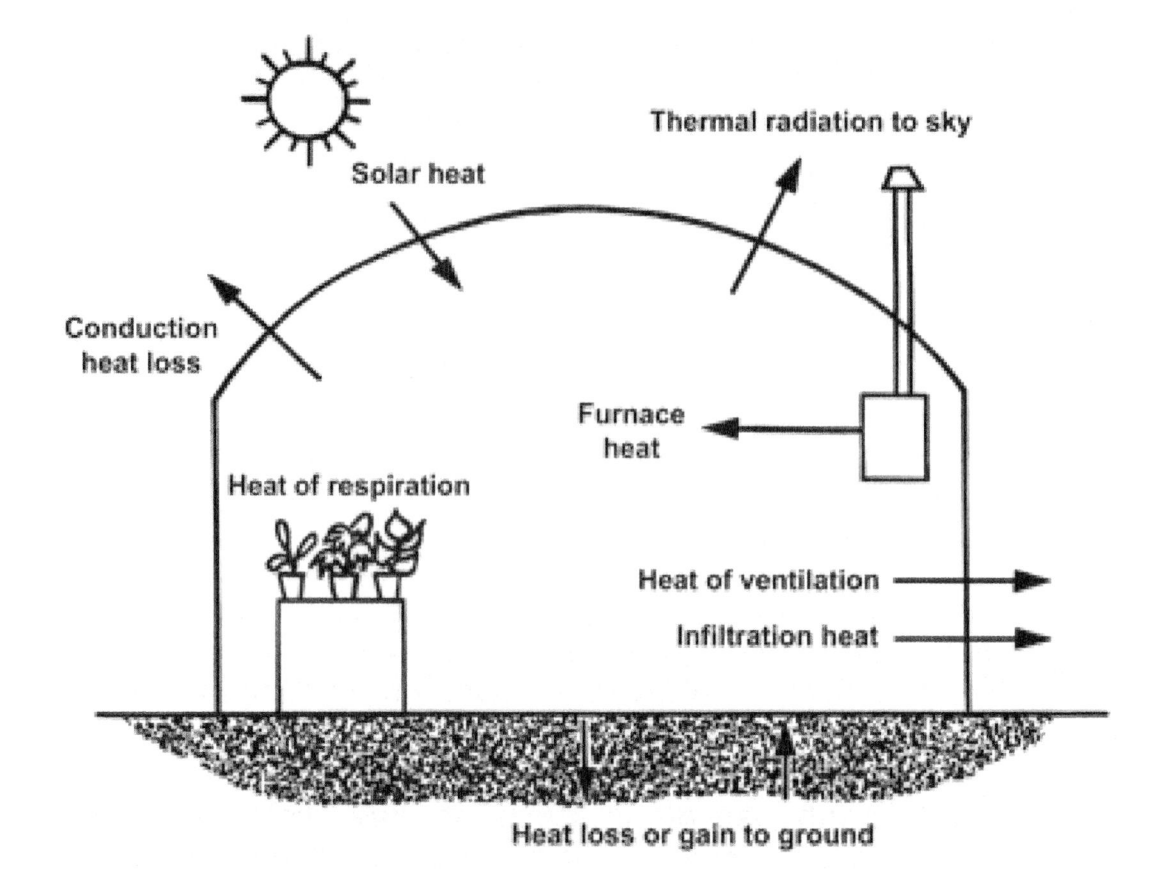

Figure 2. Energy losses and gains in a greenhouse.

Heat loss calculation

Heat loss by conduction may be estimated with the following equation:

$$Q = A(T_i - T_o)/R$$

Where:

Q = Heat loss, BTU/hr

A = Area of greenhouse surface, sq ft

R = Resistance to heat flow (a characteristic of the material)

(Ti-To) = Air temperature differences between inside and outside

Table 1 lists different materials commonly used in greenhouse construction and their associated R values. Table 1 also lists overall R values for various construction assemblies. Note that high R values indicate less heat flow. Building materials that absorb moisture will conduct heat once they are wet. Use vapor barriers to protect materials that are permeable to water vapor. Heat is also lost to the ground underneath and beside a greenhouse. The perimeter heat loss may be added to other losses using Table 1 and the equation:

Q = PL (Ti - To)

P = Perimeter heat loss coefficient, BTU/ft °F hr

L = Distance around perimeter

Table 1. Heat Flow Through Various Construction Materials and Assemblies.

Materials	R-Value
Glass fiber board, 1"	4.0
Expanded polystyrene, 1", cut surfaces	4.0
Expanded polystyrene, 1", smooth skin surface	5.0
Expanded polystyrene, molded beads, 1"	3.6
Expanded polyurethane, 1"	6.2

Vermiculite, 1"	2.2
Glass fiber blanket, 3-3.5"	11.0
Glass fiber blanket, 5.0-6.5"	19.0
Wall Materials	
Concrete block, 8"	2.00*
Plywood, ½"	1.43*
Concrete, poured, 6"	1.25*
Concrete block or plywood, plus 1" foamed urethane	7.69*
or plus 1" polystyrene	5.0*
Greenhouse with thin thermal curtains	1.42-3.33*

Construction Assemblies

Material	Overall R-Value
Roof and Wall Coverings	
Glass, single layer	0.91*
Glass, double layer, ¼" space	2.00*
Polyethylene or other film, single layer	0.83*
Polyethylene or other film, double layer separated	1.43*
Polyethylene film, double layer, separated, over glass	2.00*
Fiberglass reinforced pane	0.83*
Double acrylic or polycarbonate	2.00*
Perimeter	Btu/linear ft °F hr
Uninsulated	0.8
Insulated	0.4

> *Includes effects of surface coefficients.

Add infiltration heat losses to the conduction heat losses. The equation for infiltration heat transfer follows:

$Q = 0.02 \, V \, C \, (T_i - T_o)$

V = Greenhouse volume, cu ft

C = Number of air exchanges per hour

Table 2 lists estimates of air exchanges through types of greenhouses. The number of air exchanges per hour will vary depending on the type and condition of the greenhouse and the amount of wind.

Table 2. **Natural Air Exchanges for Greenhouses**

Construction System	Air Exchanges per Hour[1]
New Construction, glass or fiberglass	0.75 to 1
New Construction, double layer plastic film	0.5 to 1.0
Old Construction glass, good maintenance	1 to 2
Old Construction glass, poor condition	2 to 4
[1]Low wind or protection from wind reduces the air exchange rate.	

Minimum design temperature

A good outside temperature to use in heater design calculations (to select heater size) can be found by subtracting 15 degrees F from the average daily minimum January temperature (see Table 3). Another requirement the heater must meet is to provide enough heat to prevent plants from freezing during periods of extremely low temperatures. The minimum temperatures for various locations within Georgia are also shown in Table 3.

Table 3. **Climatic Conditions in Georgia (1948-2004)**

Location	Minimum Temperature °F and (Year Occurring)	Average Daily Minimum January Temperatures (°F)
Atlanta	-8 (1985)	33.6
Athens	-4 (1985)	33.2
Augusta	-1 (1985)	33.6

Columbus	-2 (1985)	36.4
Macon	-6 (1985)	35.8
Rome	-9 (1985)	30.5
Savannah	3 (1985)	39.0
Tifton	0 (1985)	38.0
Valdosta	9 (1981)	38.6

Example:

maintain a temperature of 65 degrees f inside a double layer plastic greenhouse with dimensions as shown in figure 3 with no foundation insulation. assume an augusta location.

Surface Area:			
Walls	7 x 100 x 2	=	1400.0 ft²
Roof	16.86* x 100 x 2	=	3372.0 ft²
Ends	(32 x 7 + 5.33 x 16)2	=	618.6 ft²
			5390.6 ft²

* This dimension can be determined by drawing the greenhouse cross-section to scale and measuring this length along the rafters.

At an Augusta location and an average daily minimum January temperature of 33.6 degrees F, the design temperature would be about 18.6 degrees F, so use 20 degrees F. This requires a 45-degree F rise above design temperature; and, with double layer plastic, the R-value will be 1.43.

$$= \text{Area} \times \Delta T / R$$

Conduction Heat Loss, Q_C:	= 5391.0 x 45/1.43 = 169,647 BTU/hr
Volume:	= (7 x 32 x 100) + (16 x 5.33 x 100) = 22,400 + 8,528 = 30,928 ft³
Air Infiltration Losses, Q_A:	= 0.02 x Volume x C x ΔT = 0.02 x 30,928 x 1.0 x 45 = 27,835 BTU/hr
Perimeter Heat Loss, Q_P:	= P x L x (ΔT) = 0.8 x 264 x 45 = 9,504 BTU/hr
Total Heat Loss, Q_T:	= $Q_C + Q_A + Q_P$ = 169,647 + 27,835 + 9,504
Heat Required = 206,986 BTU/hr	

The coldest temperature recorded in Augusta is -1 degree F and, with a 45-degree F temperature rise, the plants should not be in jeopardy from freezing. An increase in heat requirement of approximately 20 percent would be necessary if the house were located on a windy hill.

12"
4"
5.33'
7'
32'
100'

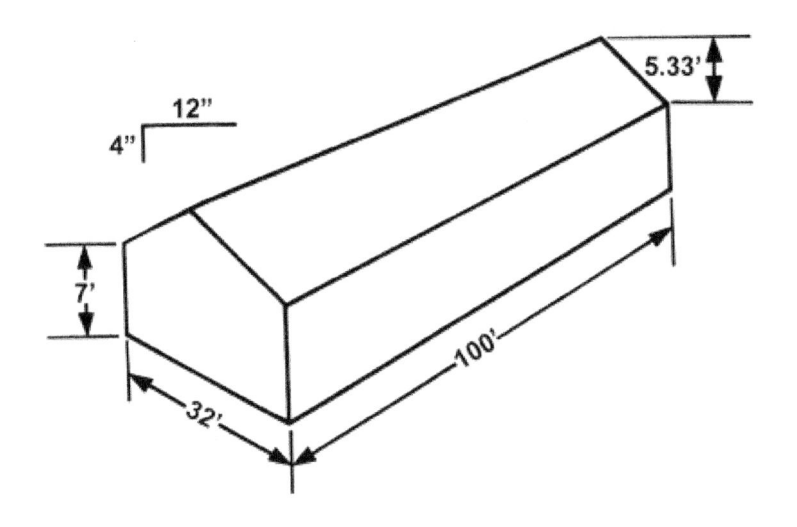

OTHER HEATING SYSTEM DESIGN CONSIDERATIONS

Plastic greenhouses often have a humidity buildup within the enclosure since almost no cracks or openings exist as in a glass house. High humidity can lead to increased occurrence of leaf and flower diseases. A forced air heating system helps mix the air within the house and helps prevent temperature variation within the house. In fact, it is desirable to have fans along the walls to circulate and mix the warm air with the cooler air near the surface. They can be operated continuously during cold periods even if the heater is not on.

Duct systems to evenly distribute the heated air from the forced warm air furnace are desirable. Two or more small heating units are preferable to one larger unit, since two units offer more protection if one unit malfunctions.

A warning device is good insurance should the heating system malfunction or if a power failure occurs. Some greenhouse operators prefer to have a battery powered alarm system to warn them if the temperature gets out of the acceptable range.

Ventilation

Ventilation reduces inside temperature during sunny days and supplies carbon dioxide, which is vital to the plants' photosynthesis. Another advantage of ventilation is to remove warm, moist air and replace it with drier air. High humidity is objectionable since it causes moisture condensation on cool surfaces and tends to increase the occurrence of diseases.

Some glass houses are ventilated by manually operated ventilators in the roof. This method is usually not satisfactory for ventilating plastic covered houses due to the rapid temperature fluctuations possible. Ventilating fans are highly recommended in Georgia.

Winter ventilation should be designed to prevent cold drafts on plants. This has been a problem with some systems using shutters at one end of a house and an exhaust fan at the other. The problem can be minimized by placing the intake high in the gable and using baffles to deflect the incoming air.

Draft-free winter ventilation can be provided by using the convection tube system, consisting of exhaust fans and fresh air inlets located in the gable and end wall. This is connected to a thin plastic tube extending the length of the greenhouse. The tube is suspended on a wire near the ridge and has holes along its entire length. The fans can be thermostatically controlled. Fan operation produces a slight air pressure drop inside the greenhouse, causing fresh air to flow into the inlet and inflate the tube, which discharges air into the house through the holes in the tube. The holes emit "jets" of air that should project horizontally to provide proper distribution and mixing with warm air before reaching the plants.

The thermostat stops the fans when the desired temperature is reached; the tube collapses and ventilation stops. In a tightly constructed greenhouse, it makes little difference where fans are located in convection tube ventilation since the air distribution is determined by the tubes. Less fan capacity is usually required for theconvection tubesystem than for any other winter ventilation system. Additional air is necessary as the outdoor temperature rises to the point where full capacity of the tube is reached. The outside air is usually warm enough by this time to be admitted through doors or other openings at plant level.

Fans may be added or possibly combined with a cooling pad for use in evaporative cooling. In fact, air may be pulled through the pad with or without water in the pad. In warm periods, enough air needs to be pulled from the house to provide a complete air exchange every 60 seconds. Control fans by a thermostat or humidistat to provide proper temperature and humidity.

Greenhouses equipped with an evaporative cooling pad system having three fans or fewer should have one fan with a two-speed motor to prevent excessive temperature fluctuationsand fan cycling. Select all fans to operate against a slight pressure (⅛ inch static water pressure). Fans not rated against slight pressure usually moveonly 60 to 70 percent of the rated air flow when installed in greenhouses. It is recommended that only fans that have been tested and their performance verified by an independent testing lab, such as AMCA, be used, since that is the only assurance that the design ventilation rate is being achieved.

Exhaust fans in end wall

Fans in the end wall (Figure 4) are the most common method of forced ventilation. The air enters through the motorized shutter (winter) and is pulled through the greenhouse by the exhaust fans.

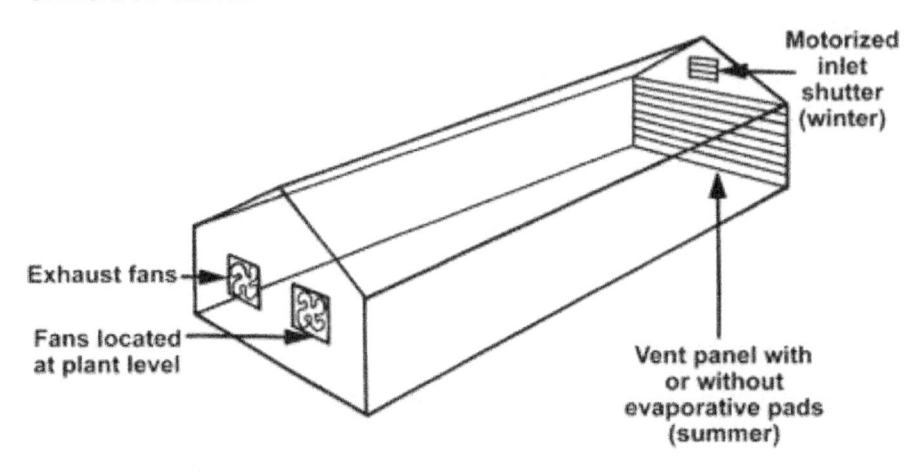

Figure 4. Fans in end wall.

The exhaust fans should be able to move small air volumes without drafts (winter) and yet provide enough fan capacity for an air exchange within the house each minute during summer. One air exchange per minute (without evaporative cooling) should keep the temperature about 8 degrees F higher than outside temperatures. One-half of this air volume will produce about a 15-degree F temperature rise, while two air exchanges per minute will cause a temperature rise of about 5 degrees F. Ideally, the length of the house should not exceed 125 feet using this method. Houses up to 250 feet long, however, have been satisfactorily ventilated using this method. Temperature variations are greater in longer houses, so higher ventilation rates are desirable. No air must be allowed to enter the house at the sides or at the fan end.

Glazing in glass houses must be well set and the houses in good repair to prevent significant quantities of air leaking into the house. If cooling pads are used during summer, disconnect the motorized shutter and close it to prevent hot air from entering through the shutter and bypassing the cooling pads. You can connect a perforated plastic tube to the same inlet shutter to provide good air distribution for cold weather ventilation.

The same principle applies for multiple ridge houses, provided each end wall is so equipped. One two-speed fan is usually used in small hobby houses.

The total inlet opening in the end wall for summer ventilation (shutter and evaporative pad vent) should provide about 1.5 square feet per 1,000 cubic feet per minute of air moving through the operating fans. The motorized shutter and one or two fans might be connected on one thermostat while the remaining fans are connected to a different thermostat, with air being supplied to these fans through the vent panel containing the evaporative pad.

Pressure fans in end walls

Ventilation for greenhouses that are 100 feet or shorter can be accomplished by mounting pressure fans, which blow air into the house, high in the end walls. See Figure 5.

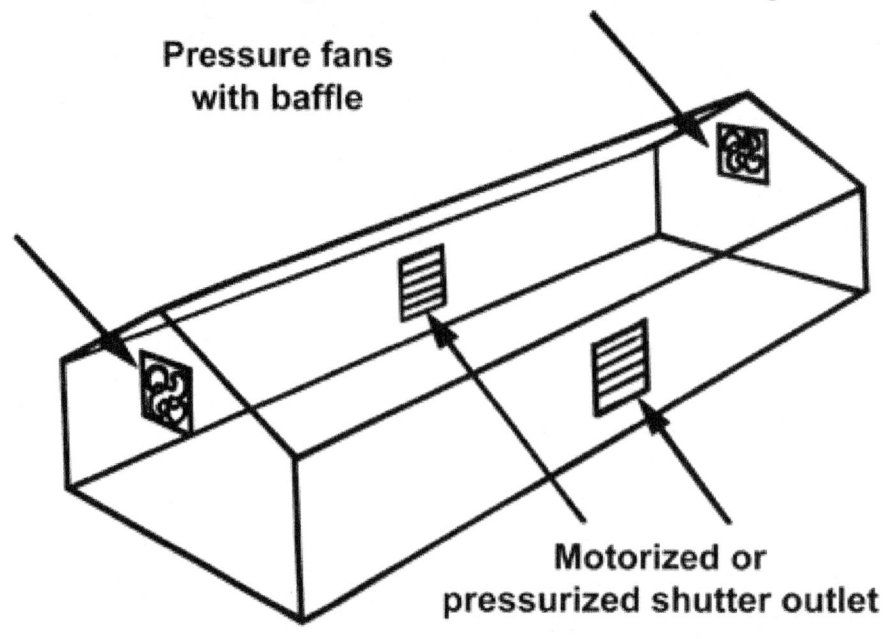

Figure 5. Pressure fans mounted high in the end walls.

The fans in the end wall are usually two-speed and controlled by separate thermostats. To avoid high velocity air striking plants, a baffle is placed in front of the fans to direct the air in the direction desired. The fans should have a protective hood to prevent rain from being blown into the house.

One pressurized system where evaporative cooling is possible is shown in Figure 6. This system places the pressure fans in the side wall. The pressurized system with fans in the side wall does not work well when the foliage is dense and lots of tall, growing plants are present. Notice the air outlet and inlet are on the same side of the house in this case, with a box enclosure around the fan where cooling pads are installed.

Evaporative cooling

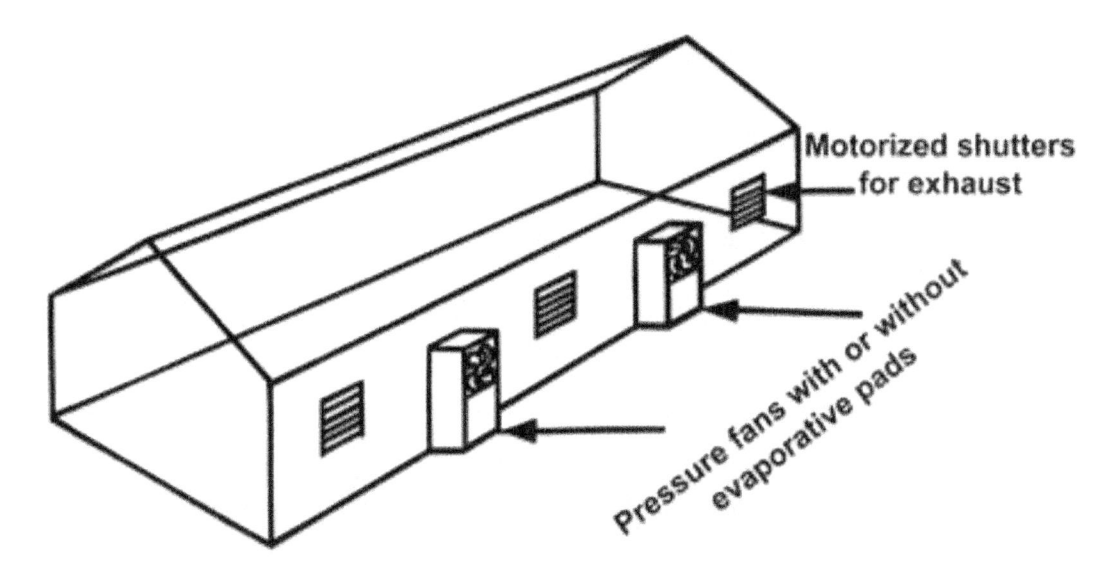

Figure 6. Pressure fans mounted in the sidewalls.

The heat absorbed on a dark surface perpendicular to the sun's rays can be as high as 300 BTU/HR per square foot of surface. So it would be possible, theoretically, for a greenhouse to absorb 300 BTUs per hour for each square foot of floor area. This excessive energy leads to heat buildup and, on warm days, can cause plants to wilt.

Excessive heat buildup can often be prevented with shading materials such as roll-up screens of wood, aluminum or vinyl plastic as well as paint-on materials (shading compounds). Roll-up screens, which work well in hobby houses, are available with pulleys and rot-resistant nylon ropes. These screen can be adjusted from outside as temperature varies. Radiation can be reduced by 50 percent with this method, which should reduce temperature rise proportionally if ventilation rate remains constant. Shading also reduces light striking the plants, which may limit their growth rate since light is essential to photosynthesis. This is a trade-off that is sometimes necessary to reduce temperatures.

If summer temperatures exceed those considered acceptable and cannot be corrected with reasonable ventilation rates and shading, the only alternative is evaporative cooling. A fan and pad system using evaporative cooling eliminates excess heat and adds humidity. This reduces plant moisture losses and, therefore, reduces plant wilting. Temperature is lowered, humidity is increased and watering needs are reduced.

An evaporative cooling system moves air through a screen or spray of water in such a manner that evaporation of water occurs. About 1,000 BTUs of heat are required to change 1 pound of water from liquid to vapor. If the heat for evaporation comes from the air, the air is cooled. Evaporation is greater when the air entering the system is dry; that is, when the relative humidity is low, allowing the air to evaporate a lot of water. The water holding ability of air is expressed in terms of relative humidity. A relative humidity of 50 percent, for example, means the air is holding one-half of the maximum water that the air could hold if saturated at a given temperature.

Theoretically air can be cooled evaporatively until it reaches 100 percent relative humidity. Practically, a good evaporative cooler can reach about 85 percent of this temperature drop. The cooling effect for 85 percent efficient evaporative coolers is shown in Table 4. Evaporative coolers are more effective when the humidity is low (Table 4). Fortunately, relative humidities are usually low during the warmest periods of the day. Solar heat entering the house offsets some of the cooling effect. A well-designed ventilation system pro-viding one air volume change per minute is essential for a good evaporative cooling system. A solar heat gain of 8-10 degrees F can be expected using one air change per minute. If the outside air were 90 degrees F and relative humidity were 70 percent, the resulting temperature within the house would be about 93 degrees F (83 degrees F from Table 4 plus 10 degrees F).

Table 4. **Cooling Capacity of 85 Percent Efficient Evaporative Coolers**

Outside Air	Relative Humidity			
	at 30%	at 50%	at 70%	at 90%
Outside Air Temperature °F	Cooled Air Temperature °F			
100	79	86	91	96
90	70	77	83	87
80	63	69	74	77
70	54	60	64	68

If a cooling efficiency of 85 percent is to be realized, at least 1 square foot of pad area (aspen fiber) mounted vertically should be provided for each 150 CFM of air circulated by the fans. Many pad materials have been used successfully, provided a complete water film does not form and block air movement through the wet pad. Table 5 gives recommended air flow through various pad type materials.

Table 5. **Recommended Airflow Rate through Various Pad Materials.**

Pad Type	Airflow Rate through Pad (CFM/ft^2)
Aspen fiber mounted vertically (2-4 in. thick)	150
Aspen fiber mounted horizontally (2-4 in. thick)	200
Corrugated cellulose (4 in. thick)	250
Corrugated cellulose (6 in. thick)	350

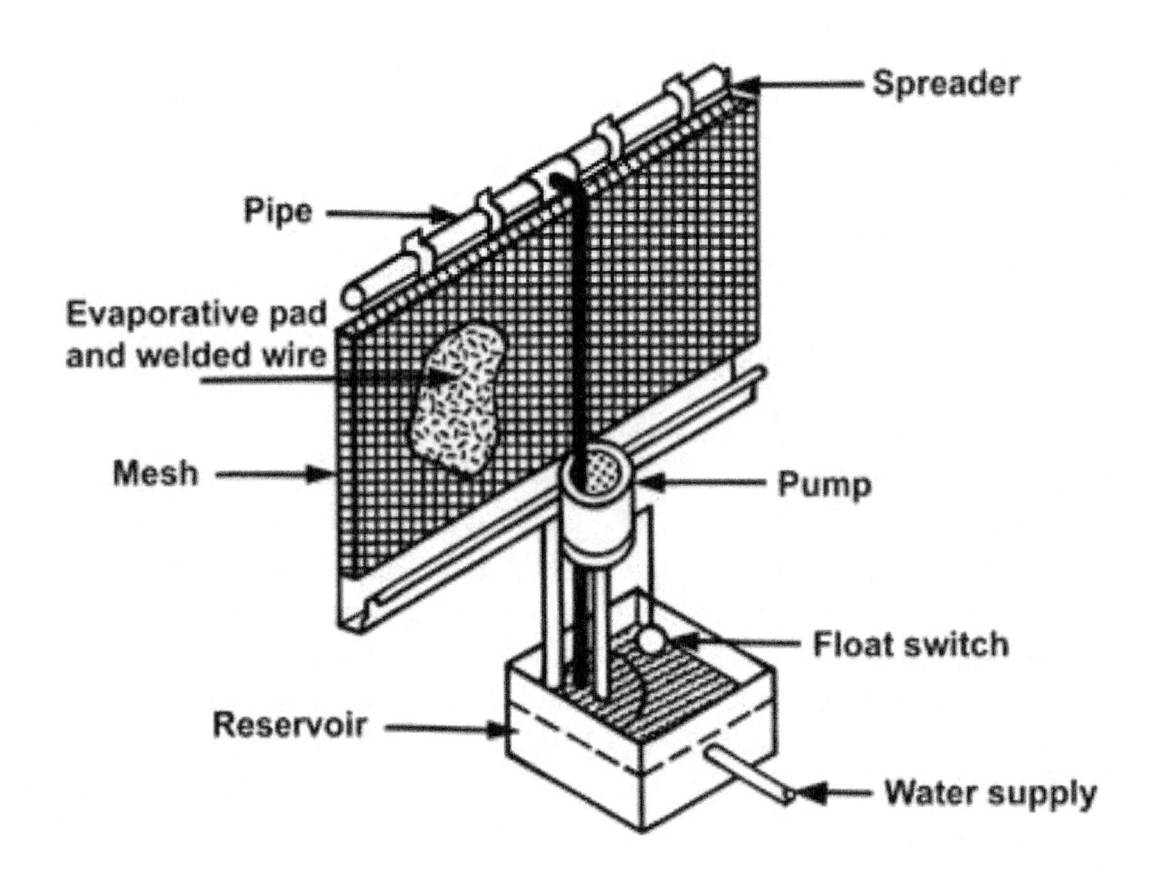

Figure 7. Typical evaporative cooling system.

Aspen pads are usually confined in a welded wire mesh. A pipe with closely spaced holes allows water to run down a sheet metal spreader onto the pads (Figure 7). The flow rate of the water supplying header pipe is listed in Table 6. Water than does not evaporate in the air stream is caught in the gutter and returned to a reservoir for recycling. The reservoir should have the capacity to hold the water returning from the pad when the system is turned off. Table 6 shows recommended reservoir capacity for different type pads.

Table 6. **Recommended Water Flow Rate and Reservoir Capacity for Vertically Mounted Cooling Pad Materials.**

Pad Type	Min. Flowrate per Length of Pad (gpm/ft)	Min. Reservoir Capacity per Unit Pad Area (Gal/ft^2)
Aspen fiber (2-4 inches)	0.3	0.5
Corrugated cellulose (4 inches)	0.5	0.8
Corrugated cellulose (6 inches)	0.8	1.0

A cover of some sort is needed to prevent air flow through the pads during cold weather. These can be manually operated or automated. Float control easily controls water supply. It is desirable to use an algaecide in the circulating water to prevent algae growth on the pads. You must, therefore, prevent rain water from entering the evaporative cooling water, causing dilution of the chemical mixture.

Evaporative pads in an endome on the suction side of fans that discharge air into houses (pressure fans) have not worked well, primarily due to the distribution of the cooled air. The same is true of package unit evaporative coolers where poor air distribution is concerned. These units can handle air volumes of 2,000 to 20,000 CFM. The problem with them is the difficulty providing uniform cooled air distribution. The closer the units are spaced along the walls, the better the air distribution will be. Package coolers have been used in small houses, and in houses with good air distribution, with considerable success. The pressurized system forces air, which must displace air within the house, into the greenhouse. Vents must be provided for air circulation.

Mist cooling

Evaporative cooling by spraying tiny water droplets into the greenhouse has met with limited success. The droplets must be tiny, and this requires tiny, closely spaced nozzles operated at relatively high pressures an expensive design. Water must be well filtered to prevent nozzles from clogging. Uniform distribution of the water droplets throughout the house is difficult to accomplish.

If the mist system carries any minerals in the water, deposits will be left on plant foliage. This accumulation can reduce photosynthesis substantially and can lead to salt toxicity. The mist system can also cause wet foliage, leading to disease problems, particularly when the droplet size is too large.

Mist cooling does not cool as effectively as a conventional evaporative cooling pad system but it is less expensive. The system requires no collection pan or sump. It can cause runoff or puddling beneath the pads if all the water sprayed on the pads is not vaporized.

A system that is actually a combination of a cooling pad and misting (or fogging) system is shown in Figure 8. This is sometimes called a "fogging pad" system. Some growers have used it with success

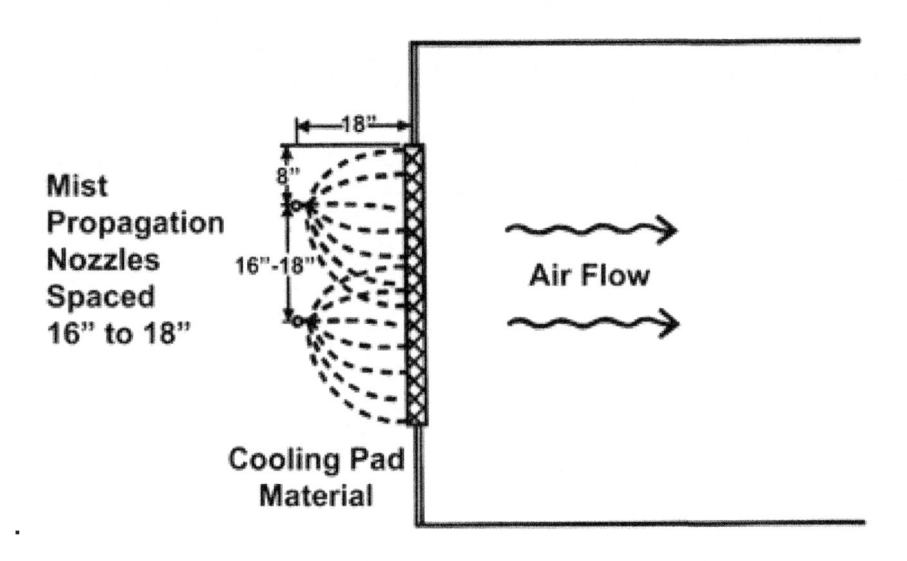

Figure 8. Mist nozzle used as evaporative cooling.

The system should provide approximately 20 gallons of water per minute to be sprayed on the pad (typically 20, 1-gpm spray nozzles) for each 48-inch fan in the ventilation system. This amount of water, however, will not always be needed.

Warmer air will evaporate water faster than cooler air. The amount of water added to the pads can be adjusted using a combination of valves, time clocks and thermostats. As the temperature in the greenhouse increases, so does the frequency of mist nozzle operation.

HOW TO IRRIGATE YOUR GREENHOUSE TO REDUCES THE AMOUNT OF PLANT LOSS CAUSED BY STRESS INDUCED BY DELIVERING AN INCONSISTENT AMOUNT OF WATER OR FERTILIZER

The industry's most reliably successful growers are increasingly automating their irrigationsystems for the significant improvements it makes to both their efficiency and crop quality. When a machine runs irrigation, plants receive a consistent amount of water, which makes the crop much more uniform. Irrigation consistency also reduces theamount of plant losscaused by stress induced by delivering an inconsistent amount of water or fertilizer.

Larger growers have been among the first to adopt these methods because of the capital costs, but small- to medium-sized growers also are realizing opportunities to automate on a tight budget. For example, in a typical 30×96-foot greenhouse, basic overhead irrigation can be installed for as little as $325. That's certainly not a budget limited to big growers. This inexpensive entry investment allows growers more free time while machines take care of their plants. Even at that cost, a smart grower would run the numbers to determine whether the system made financial sense for him. Applying 1 inch of water to that typical greenhouse requires 1,795 gallons of water, which would take 4.3 hours using a nozzle with a typical 7 gallons per minute output _Ñ assuming perfect labor efficiency. At minimum wage, that's $36 per watering, so the $325 investment is recouped in nine waterings. Run the numbers for your own operation to see how the economics work for you.

There are six ways to irrigate your greenhouse, but choosing the wrong system for your operation and crops can lead to big issues. Use the following guide, compiled by the experts at McConkey Company, to help you choose.

Each of these irrigation methods are a delivery mechanism for water, but they still require a corresponding controller to regulate when and how much to water. Controllerscan be assimpleas $45 units that switch on the system at certain times of the dayand as advanced as units that sense solar heat, air humidity and soil moisture.

1 Drip Systemsfor Hanging Baskets

Drip systems are intravenous tubes feeding directly to each emitter from a main supply line running the length of the bay. Hanging baskets are one of the first crops growers choose to automate with drip irrigation. Drip systems help reduce disease by keeping plants' foliage dry.With this system, the drippers turn on and off in unison, even if the greenhouse is sloped or the lines are uneven. The drip emitters are pressure compensated so the entire line of hanging baskets will be irrigated with equal amounts of water. Dripperscome preassembled in various lengths to accommodate varioussuspension heights in greenhouses. Baskets up to 12 inchesare ideally suited for dripsystems. Larger baskets may require spray stakesor several emittersper basket.

2 Drip or Spray Stakes for Potted Crops and Nursery Containers

Potted crops or outdoor nursery containers can also be watered automatically with drip emitters or spray stakes.

Drippers are used on smaller containers from 31/2 square inches up to gallon and larger containers. Small containers allow the dripping water to migrate outward and saturate the soil profile. For larger containers, spray stakes help convey water across the soil surface area for adequate saturation. Drip systems and spray stake sensure the water is injected directly to the soil, which reduces over spray.

3 Microsprinklers (Overhead)

Microsprinklers simulate a light rain or mist. They are typically installed overhead and are ideally suited for flat material such as cell packs or square containers. Any crop grown edge toedge in a greenhouse and not sensitive to wetting foliage is a good candidate for microsprinklers. With their low cost and easy setup, overhead systems are among the most popular and offer one of the quickest returns on investment. They can be set up to irrigate the entire greenhouse area or be zoned to water different crops at different timesand rates.

4 Ebb-and-Flood Systems, Capillary Mats

Ebb-and-flood systems and capillary mats both water from the bottom up instead of overhead.Crops sensitive to overhead watering, or those whose foliage creates a barrier to overhead watering, lend themselves to bottom watering.Ebb-and-flood systems are typically closed-loop systems where the water is applied, reclaimed, treated and reapplied to crop. These systems carry the risk of spreading disease, as infected plants' water can drain out and into nearby healthy plants. Capillary mats require good aeration to prevent algae buildup because they do not drain dry between irrigation cycles.These systems minimize foliar disease because foliage stays dry, which allows for lower greenhouse temperatures and lower fuel costs in some situations.

5 Drip Tape

Originally used outdoors in field crops or orchards, drip tape has found a home in greenhouses. Because a variety of differently spaced, pressure-compensated emitters can be embedded into the drip tape, crops from poinsettias to mums to larger flowering annuals are now being irrigated in this way. Drip tape is ideal when larger numbers of a particular crop are being grown in 6-inch or larger material. The location of each emitter is marked on the drip tape to make positioning the pot under the tape quick and easy, which saves up to 20 percent in installation labor over drip tubes. Drip tape also helps keep foliage dry, thus reducing the risk of disease.

6 Boom Irrigation

With boom irrigation systems, a grower can apply water in precise amounts not possible with other systems. Precision of quantity is essential during propagation, whether from seed, plugs or cuttings. Booms provide quicker rooting, better growth, more uniform growth and less crop loss, mainly because the amount of water being delivered can be controlled and is being delivered more uniformly. Plug growers will irrigate with little else: Because of their small volume, plug cells dry out faster and require multiple waterings each day. Consider a 512-cell plug tray with 0.14 fluid ounces per cell empty. With just a few extra drops of more water in one cell than an adjacent cell, they will have drastically varying amounts of water and consequently their growth will not be uniform. Booms help avoid this issue and are ideal for any greenhouse crop (grown edge to edge) that is not sensitive to wetting foliage. Growers can water just to the leach point to save on fertilizer costs, or they can water just the top soil profile for newly transplanted material to save on water and fertilizer. Advanced boom controllers can change watering zones throughout a greenhouse, which saves growers water by not watering unplanted areas of a greenhouse.

Boom controllers in the past have been criticized as difficult to program, but growers are finding a new generation of easy-to-use, touchscreen controllers that allow for quicker training and fast staff adoption. When choosing a boom system, be sure to interact with thesystems under consideration to evaluate how well they will be used after their installation, and gather feedback from any staff that will be using the system.

HOW TO SAVOID WIND DAMAGE FOR YOUR GREENHOUSE

Hereare some helpful hintsand tips to help you avoid any storm damage this winter.

ALL greenhouses are particularly vulnerable to wind damage, and even more so when new.

Of course, some modelsare stronger in the wind, but they are ALL vulnerable to wind damage EVEN THE VERY STRONGEST MODELS AVAILABLE IN BRITAIN. So we recommend that you take the potential threat of the wind to damage your greenhouse veryseriously not just when choosing your greenhouse, but also positioning it, maintaining it and checking it on an ongoing basis.

Severe winds are so much more common nowadays he kind of wind which we used to see onceevery 10 years, now seems tocome more than once a year!

To help prevent panes of glass blowing out and to minimise the risk of moreserious damage follow thesesteps:

• Position your greenhouse in a position that isas sheltered from the wind aspossible. Consider planting hedges or positioning fences as protection from the winds in the future.

• Go for thestrongest greenhouseyou can afford: as a general rule, the moreyou spend (on the basic

frame- not your total bill), the stronger the frame will be. Consider bar capping to replace clips if it is available.

• If your glass is held in with clips, your greenhouse is most vulnerable topanesof glass blowing out in high winds. To helpprevent this, we recommend using siliconesealant tosecure the clips (click here to view a help sheet on this topic).

• Alternatively, if you have a Simplicity greenhouse, you can replace the clips with Bar capping, a full length PVC capping system that secures the glassall the way upand holds it far more firmly in windy conditions.

• Make sureyour greenhouse is anchored down to the floor assecurelyaspossible. If your greenhouse is on slabs or concrete; drill and screw it down with brown Rawl plugsand 2" no 10 screws using a 7mm hammer drill bit.

• Makesure that your greenhouse is attached properly toyour metal base (if applicable). Although some basescome with metal 'J-clips' to attach them to the greenhouse, if you live in windyconditions, we recommend that you drill through the sill of the greenhouse, through the baseand bolt them together with a standard greenhouse bolt and nut. Do this about every 2-4' around the greenhouse. Thisprovides a good extra precaution. (Takecare if you do this before glazing that your bolt head will not be in the way of the glass).

• Shelter your greenhouse by situating fences or hedging in the way of theprevailing winds. Also beaware that areas that look 'sheltered' may in fact be 'wind tunnels' (e.g down thesideof a house). This is very important.

• Before heavy winds, make sure that your doorsand windows are closed and will stayclosed during the wind. If you have a sliding door that has nocatch to keep it closed, then you can secure it by drilling a hole in the top door track and inserting a padlock.

• After heavy winds, check your greenhouse. You may find that someclips have moved and got behind the glassand are not securing it - this may weaken the fixing of thepane, then later it may blow out in a comparatively mild wind. These clips need repositioning as soon as possible and to help keep them in place you can put somesiliconearound them. Likewise you may even have had a pane blow out and without checking you may never realise it: this is a dangeroussituation because there is a gap in the greenhouse and if the wind gets upagain it could causesome more damage quickly.

HOW TO GROW TOMATOES, PEPPER AND TROPICAL FRUITS IN A GREENHOUSE

tomatoes are the most popular greenhouse crop on the planet. With good temperature control and plenty of light, greenhouse growers in most areas of the world can get two tomato crops per year. Indoor conditions do require more careful handling to prevent diseaseand successfully pollinate the flowers.

Setting

1 heck temperature. Tomatoes grow best at daytime temperatures of 70 to 80° F (21–27° C), and nighttime temperatures of 60–65° F (16–18° C).[2][3] Make sure you can maintain these temperatures in your greenhouse for several months before you plant.

• Ideally, bring temperatures to the lower end of this range on overcast days, and raise them to the upper end (or even slightly higher) during clear, sunny days.

• You'll also need to keep humidity below 90% to prevent excessive leaf mold. Ventilate regularly to bring fresh, dry air into the greenhouse, especially on cool, cloudy mornings.

2 Select a tomato variety. There are thousands of tomato varieties, so for detailed information it's best to talk to local growers. There are a few guidelines and tips that apply to all regions, however:

- Tomatoes marketed as greenhouse varieties are more tolerant of greenhouse conditions.

- The letters VFNT and A after the name mean the variety is resistant to disease.

- "Indeterminate" tomatoes grow and produce fruit indefinitely, taking advantage of the longer growing season inside a greenhouse. If you're short on space, plant a "determinate" variety, which stops at a certain height.

3 Choose a growing medium. Tomatoes can grow in any well-draining material. You can use your preferred soil-less mix, or one of these options:

- Perlite bags or rock wool slabs are the cheapest options in many areas.

- Some growers prefer a 1:1 mix of sphagnum peat moss and vermiculite.

- Purchase sterile soil mix or make your own. Never use soil or compost from your garden without sterilizing. Choose this option if you do not want to install an irrigation system.

4 Install an irrigation system (recommended). Most growers install drip tubing to deliver water to each plant. A fertilizer injector attached to the tubing can automate fertilizing as well.

- Tomatoes are also easy to grow in a hydroponics system. See this article for detailed instructions.

Planting

1 Fill a starting tray with potting mix. Wash the tray thoroughly with soap and water to disinfect it. Fill the tray with any of the potting mixes described above.

• If you use soil, make sure it is sterile.

• If you use a soil-less mix, you'll also need a seedling nutrient solution (see below).

2 Plant each seed in its own cup. Poke a ¼ inch (6 mm) hole into each compartment of the starting tray. Drop a single seed into each hole. Cover lightly with the potting mix.

• Plant about 10-15% more seeds than you plan on growing, so you can discard the least healthy seedlings.

3 Moisten with water or dilute nutrient solution. Use plain water for soil, or seedling nutrient solution for soil-less mixes. Either way, water until the mixture is just damp enough to press into a clump, with only a few drops squeezed out. Water regularly to keep the mix damp.

• A 5:2:5 nutrient solution that contains calcium and magnesium is ideal. Dilute the solution according to label instructions.

4 Keep the tray on a warm windowsill. Do not bring the seeds into the greenhouse until they've sprouted, so you can check for disease and pests. Provide plenty of sunlight and keep the temperature at 75–80° F (24–27° C) during the day.

• To keep temperatures under control, you may want to start the tray in partial sun. Move to full sun once all seedlings have sprouted. This usually takes 5 to 12 days.

5 Transplant to larger containers. Transplant the seedlings to small pots in the greenhouse about two weeks after they emerge. After six to eight weeks, or once seedlings are 4-6 inches (10–15 cm) tall, transplant them to larger pots or bags. A typical plant needs roughly ½ to 1 cubic foot of potting material (3.7–7.5 gallons, or 14–28 liters) Even smaller varieties may produce less fruit if grown in smaller pots.

• If you see any insects, mold, or disease spots on a plant, do not bring any of them to the greenhouse.

• Give each plant about 4 square feet (0.37 m2) of floor space. Planting too close together can reduceairflow and encourage disease.

6 Adjust pH and calcium levels. Before the final transplant, you may want to check soil pH, which ideally falls between 5.8 and 6.8.If your soil is too acidic, add about 1 tsp (5 mL) hydrated lime for each gallon (3.8 L) of potting mix. Besides raising the pH, this adds calcium that can prevent blossom rot later on.

• If your pH is fine, mix in gypsum or calcium sulfate instead to add calcium without changing the pH.[19] Alternatively, just choose a fertilizer that contains calcium and apply every week or two.

• In a hydroponics setup, you can supply calcium by injecting calcium nitrate into the irrigation feed. This requires a second injector, as calcium nitrate cannot be stored with your main fertilizer.

Caring For The Plant

1 Fertilize regularly. Start fertilizing the day you transplant the tomatoes into their final pot. Use a complete fertilizer high in nitrogen (N) and potassium (K), such as a 15-5-15 or 5-2-5. Dilute and apply the fertilizer according to label instructions.

• Reduce fertilizer as the final fruits ripen. Do not fertilize in late autumn or winter, unless using artificial grow lights and reliable heater.

2 Remove suckers weekly. Once a week, pinch off "suckers," or side shoots that emerge where a leaf meets the main stem. Leave only the main bud at the top of the steam, plus the highest sucker below it. This trains the plant to grow upward instead of wide.

- If the top of your plant is damaged, the top sucker can become the new main stem.

3 Stake the tomato plants. Tie the plants loosely to stakes with twine to keep them upright as they grow. Use plastic garden clips where necessary to secure the twine.

- In peak growing season, the plant will grow up to 6 in (15 cm) per week and will need tying each week.

- Commercial operations save on materials by stringing a wire over each row, with a support post every 20 ft (6m). Wrap the twine around each plant and fasten to the overhead wire.

- For smaller home gardens, you can place a tomato cage over each plant when it is small. These don't require as much maintenance as staking.

4 Pollinate the flowers. Unlike many plants, a tomato can pollinate itself but it needs some help. The pollen in a tomato flower is trapped inside a tube, and must be released through vibration. Since most greenhouses lack bees or high wind, you'll need to act as the pollinator once flowers are fully open:

- For best results, buy an electric plant vibrator. Touch the vibrator against each flower stalk every other day, at any time between 10am and 2pm. (An electric toothbrush is another, less effective option.)

- Alternatively, you can place fans in the greenhouse and direct the airflow over your plants to distribute the pollen.

- Large operations should consider keeping their own bees.

- Hand out cotton swabs to your children or family members and have them rub the cotton swabs in the flowers to distribute pollen.

5 Prune leaves and fruit. Apart from weekly sucker removal, pruning is not necessary until the plant starts to fruit:

- Once fruit starts to grow, thin each cluster down to four or five fruits, removing the smallest or most misshapen. Very large fruits or winter conditions may require going down to three per cluster. Varieties with small fruits may not need any thinning.

- As the fruit matures, snap off older leaves from the lower clusters. This helps improve air circulation.

6 Harvest as late as possible. The longer the tomatoes stay on the vine, the fuller and redder they become. Commercial growers typically pick a little early, when the fruit is 60–90% red, to allow for time in shipping.

How to grow pepper

Sow seeds in desired medium 6–8 weeks prior to transplanting. Maintain a constant 80–90°F (27–32°C) soil temperature. When first true leaves just show, transplant the seedlings into cell-type containers or blocks. 2" or larger containers will produce larger, stronger root systems; 4" blocks are the standard. Grow plants at 70–74°F (21–23°C) days and 68°F (20°C) nights. Fertilize with a complete nutrient solution (EC 1.5–2, pH 5.2) or equivalent as needed to keep plants dark green and healthy. When transplanting into the greenhouse, maintain temperatures of 73°F (23°C) days and 70°F (21°C) nights for the week after transplanting. This promotes rapid vegetative growth and root establishment. 7–10 days after transplanting, lower temperatures to 63–64°F (17–18°C) nights and 73–75°F (23–24°C) days. For two-stemmed plants, use a plant density of 3–3 1/2 plants/square meter, which results in 6–7 stems/square meter (9 sq.ft.). Plants can be pruned to 4 stems, maintaining 6–7 stems/square meter (9 sq.ft.), but fruit will be smaller. Remove flowers up to the second or third node after initial branching to allow the plant to reach a suitable size before trying to support a fruit load.

TRELLISING: We recommend pruning the plants to 2–4 stems and trellising them up a string, like greenhouse tomatoes.:Harvest peppers when they are 80% or more final ripe color.

DISEASES AND PESTS: Use crop rotation or new media to reduce soilborne disease problems. Use regularly scheduled releases of beneficial insects to control pests.

DAYS TO MATURITY:From transplanting.

SEED SPECS:SEEDS/OZ.: 3,200-4,150 (avg. 3,700).

TRANSPLANTS:Avg. 950 plants/1,000 seeds.

MINI:10 seeds.

PACKET:25 seeds.

HOW TO PLANT GRAPES IN A GREENHOUSE

There are actually three ways of planting grapes in a greenhouse – for larger greenhouses you can plant the grape with the root outside, or with it inside. Planting in a tub is better for small greenhouses or where you would like a number of grape varieties in a bigger greenhouse. Let's first take a look at planting with the root outside.

With this method, the vine is planted outside, and then trained into the greenhouse. This is done either by removing a brick in the bottom of the greenhouse and training it through, or using a hole in the top of the greenhouse and leading the vine in.

Grapevines have very extensive root systems, so planting with the root outside allows the root to expand and seek the moisture and nutrients it needs, potentially meaning that you won't have to water the roots yourself as often. If you don't have much space in your greenhouse, this method may be preferable, as it allows you more space in the greenhouse itself.

If you're unable or don't wish to make a hole in the greenhouse to train the grapevine through, it's also possible to grow with the root inside.

GROWING WITH THE ROOTS INSIDE

There's also the option to plant in a border or container, with the roots inside the greenhouse. This method benefits from warmer soil, which may contribute to earlier growth, but note that as it's inside, the plant will require irrigation and greater attention and care from yourself.

PLANTING IN A TUB

Vines like to grow and grow so they can quickly take over a small greenhouse. Planting in a tub checks their growth by limiting the ability of the roots to spread. Make sure that the chosen tub has adequate drainageand is filled with good quality compost. They will also need to be fed occasionally and will need to be regularly watered.

One advantage of growing in a tub is that they can be taken outside when the crop has finished. Vines themselves are quite hardy, the greenhouse is used to boost the fruiting of the grapes. Ruthless pruning down to just 4 – 6 stubs will ensure the vine does not go wild the next year.

CARING FOR GRAPES IN A GREENHOUSE

Just before growing starts in the Spring, sprinkle the rooting area with bonemal and fertiliser, and feed every three weeks once they have begun to grow. Once the grapes get their colour and have started ripening, stop feeding them, to ensure they retain the best possible taste.

Water the grapevines every seven to ten days during the growing season (more frequently if they are in tubs), but remember that outdoor roots will require less water (unless you're experiencing a spell of dry weather).

The grapes may need a hand with pollination once the vine comes into flower. You can do this by hand-pollinating them with a feather, or by shaking the stems when the greenhouse is particularly warm and well-ventilated. Either method will help with transferring pollen between the flowers.

Grapes grown in a greenhouse will require pruning, just like outdoor grapes. For grapes grown under glass, the rod and spur system is usually used, whereas the Guyot system tends to be used for outdoor-grown grapes. This article from RHS goes into a lot more detail on pruning grapes, and is worth a read.

In terms of diseases, powdery mildew can affect grapes, often brought about by poor air circulation, heat and crowding. There are a few varieties of grape that are mildew-resistant, or you can stay on top of pruning to ensure the plant doesn't get too overcrowded. Alternatively, you could use a suitable fungicide. Growing cucumbers in a greenhouse

Growing cucumbers, like European cucumbers, can be a bumper crop in greenhouses. They differ from other types of cucumbers in many ways. The fruits are long, between 14-18 inches, and weigh a pound or more each. The forest green skin is very soft, so many producers wrap each cucumber individually to protect them from bruising and to preserve freshness. The fact that they're seedless does make them easier to digest, but in reproduction terms, they are hybrids. Many years of plant breeding have resulted in vigorous, high yielding, good tasting fruits.

Even more important for growing cucumbers in a greenhouse, fruit set happens without pollination! Now greenhouse growers incorporate pollinating insects into their community. But for those of you who do not, European cucumbers can be a perfect crop for all garden zones.

Many of the varieties are described as gynoecious (all female flowers). It's a desirable characteristic because only female flowers develop into fruits. Unfortunately, a small percentage of male flowers will tag along, especially during cool weather conditions. If pollinating insects do inhabit your greenhouse, male flowers must be pinched off to prevent fruit distortion. Distinguishing male from female is very simple. The female will have a small, undeveloped sprout of fruit directly behind the flower. The male flower lacks the swollen carpel and its bloom will be darker than the female bud.

Seeds for European cucumbers can be obtained from most mail order seedhouses, including the top seed companies. There are some facts to consider before ordering: one plant should yield between 20-50 cucumbers; that's a lot of fruit. And seeds are viable for three years or more under proper storage conditions.

Growing Cucumbers in a Greenhouse: Starting Seeds and Maintaining Temperature

We sow European cucumbers around the first of February when our greenhouse environment is more spring-like. One seed per 3-inch peat pot will provide enough room for early plant development. Keep soil temperature at a consistent 65-70°F.and seeds should germinate in 3-4 days. The soil should be moist but never soggy. Make sure you sow cucumbers in peat pots and not in flats because cucurbit root systems should not be disrupted. Once the seedlings have sprouted with a couple of true leaves showing, plant the entire cucumber, peat pot and all, into the soil beds.

Seedless cucumbers demand arm temperatures for highest yields. At sowing time, soil temperatures should not dip below 68°F.

A seed germinating chamber or box will offer your seeds uniform temperatures for a healthy start. Place a soil thermometer in the area where cucumbers will be set out. When the daily reading indicates 60 degrees F. or higher, transplant your crop. If your soil temperature drops below 60°F, plant growth will stop and general vigor will deteriorate. The recommended spacing is 24 inches between each plant and 5 feet between rows. Organic hydroponic cucumbers may have a denser planting.

This crop will grow best when midday temperatures range between 70-80°F. On clear sunny days, air temperature can rise to the warmer end of the scale. Optimum nighttime temperatures should remain at 65°F, even though some varieties will tolerate a cooler night.

Have your trellis constructed and placed when cucumbers are set out. If it is only one to two large container plantings, train them up a vertical beam with nylon or plastic twine as a leader. Consider that there could be more than 15 pounds of cucumber plant on each string. The vining plant travels quickly and lateral growth requires careful pruning. Pinch off suckers (lateral growth) at the first six leaf axils. The following 8-10 shoots should be trimmed back to one leaf. The remainder can be pruned to two leaves with weaker growth allowing three leaves. Usually plants are grown up to eight feet, and are then trained back down to the ground.

When growing cucumbers, high yields depend upon a balanced diet. European cucumbers require frequent watering and plenty of nitrogen (N). Every 3 or 4 weeks, apply a compost side dressing around the base of each plant. Supplement this feeding schedule with foliar feeding using a micronutrient fish/seaweed sprayed every 14 days. Symptoms of poor nutrition could be yellow leaves, undeveloped or aborted fruit or fruit losing its color. Often you may harvest 5 or 6 cukes per plant at one time.

Growing Cucumbers in a Greenhouse: Concerns About Diseases and Insects

Growing cucumbers in a greenhouse will reduce some of the risk of diseases and insects harming your crop. Of course, a few insects and diseases could put a crimp in your cucumbers' development. Greenhouse whitefly is a potential pest in spring and summer months. Adults are easy to spot but seeing immature larvae needs the aid of a lens. An integrated control method of trapping adults with sticky orange yellow boards and a biological control agent can provide tremendous control.

If leaves begin to show a bronze, mottling discoloration, check cucumber plants for the two-spotted spider mite. All stages of the mite's life cycle are microscopic, but you may notice their webbing between stem and leaf. Safer's insecticidal soap will check populations.

A common disease affecting European cucumbers is botrytis, a fungal disease that shows as a grayish white on top of the leaves.Botrytis spreads quickly in cool, humid environments.

Powdery mildew is another disease to watch out for. It looks like a white velvet blanket on leaf tops. Powdery mildew affects most plants in the fall when temperatures drop and the relative humidity rises. Mineral fungicides may be applied with discretion at first signs of this fungus problem. Or, better yet, use AQ10 biofungicide. This is a unique biofungicide developed specifically for controlling powdery mildew on vegetables, pome and stone fruit trees, vines and other crops. AQ10 biofungicide is a water-dispersible granule formulation that contains the hyper parasite Ampelomyces as its active ingredient.

Of course, natural pesticides for garden pests are always an option.

Growing Cucumbers in a Greenhouse: Training Cucumbers

There are two methods for training vines when growing cucumbers in a greenhouse.

First, triple stem training method. With this method all the suckers are pinched off the developing vine up to the top of the trellis. At the top of the trellis bar, pinch the terminal buds of the main stem and allow three suckers to take over.

The other method is lateral growth training, all suckers are pinched off for the first 4 to 5 fruit sets. Then, the following 8 to 10 suckers are allowed to develop one leaf and one flower. Now pinch tip growth of sucker. All remaining suckers above the 8 to 10 should develop two leaves and flowers. Then pinch remaining growth. Trellis bar is approximately six feet above the ground.

Growing tropical fruit in a greenhouse

You want ant the beauty of the tropics in your own garden? You can have it... but it'll take some work. Tropical plants need warmth, sunlight, moisture... a pretty high maintenance bunch we might say. And given winter's cold, dry environment, those needs are not easy ones to deliver, unless growing inside a well-maintained greenhouse. But by doing proper research into the unique needs of the plants you wish to grow and with proper maintenance, you'll find it is possible to grow tropical vegetation in a greenhouse. Here are a few suggestions to help get you started.

Move plants around – Take special note of which plants need sunlight or shade. Make use of trays that will allow you to shift your plants throughout the garden greenhouse as necessary while allowing for proper water drainage. Also remember that some tropical crops, like the ficus, palms, or banana trees, need plenty of space to grow.

Maintain proper temperatures and air flow – Tending to tropical plants in a greenhouse requires special attention to the necessary growing temperatures and the required air flow to keep the air moist without growing molds. This is challenging to manage as you need to keep the greenhouse at a certain temperature generally between 65 to 85 degrees

Fahrenheit while never dropping below 40 degrees while also providing satisfactory air circulation.

Rainforest environment – A mister system may also come in handy to keep your tropical vegetation at the correct humidity and maintain the required rainforest environment.

Consistent watering – Growing tropical plants in the greenhouse will also take consistent watering. Generally, every other day, though watering needs will depend on the kind of plants you're growing. Here it is vital that you pay attention to your garden greenhouse temperatures and how rapidly it takes for your soil to dry. Higher temperatures mean soil should be watered more often to take care of a moist growing medium.

Clean plants – Keep plants thoroughly clean. Manage them properly by trimming lifeless material and inspecting them for pests. Handle these problems quickly to prevent them from scattering disease to other plants in the greenhouse. Moldscan bean especiallychallenging problem when trying to grow tropical plants in a greenhouseand should beeradicated quickly when seen.

Lighting Try several different lighting options in your garden greenhouse. Some tropical plants favor artificial or indirect lighting, and some are great with the filtered natural light produced by greenhouse panels. Do your homework before selecting various species of tropical plants to identify a combination that works best in your greenhouse garden.

There's a lot to manage when raising tropical plants in a greenhouse environment, but the incentive in the long run will be the total satisfaction that comes with growing lovely plants that you don't typically see in cold weather conditions.

FRUIT AND VEG GROWING CALENDAR

If you thought that growing your own fruit and was a fair-weather hobby, think again! You can take steps all year round to make your plot a fertile one and to give your plants the best possible chance of producing a successful crop. This calendar enables you to remember all those little things that go towards making your year in the garden a productive one.

JANUARY

• Concentrate on indoor activities if the weather is wet. Get your seeds ordered, browse catalogues for fruit trees and bushes, and even buy your fertiliser, sprays and pots. January is a quiet time in garden centres and they often have sales, so getting supplies in now can save you money.

• In the greenhouse, get clean labels and pots ready for sowing and check that your propagator and heater work if you don't heat it all winter.

• Pick your winter crops such as Brussels sprouts cabbages, and leeks. As soon as the soil is clear, dig it over.

• Buy your seed potatoes and start to sprout them. January is still early to sow most vegetable seeds but you can sow your first onions now.

FEBRUARY

• Try to complete all your digging this month so the soil has a chance to benefit from frost breaking it up.

• In the greenhouse or on the windowsill you can sow more seeds this month such as tomatoes, onions, celery and peppers.

• Cover rhubarb with a large, upturned pot to encourage tender new growth.

• Plant fruit trees and bushes when the soil isn't frozen.

• Cover areas of soil to be sown with seeds next month with black plastic or fleece to warm it and prevent it from getting too wet.

MARCH

• When the weather is warm and the soil is drying out a bit, you can sow lots of seeds outside. In the greenhouse and on the windowsill, March is the main month for sowing many crops.

• Dig up the last of the overwintered crops such as parsnips and leeks.

• Plant asparagus in well-prepared soil that you've cleared of weeds.

• Towards the end of the month you can plant out the first potatoes. Also plant onion sets, shallots, garlic and Jerusalem artichokes.

• Apply fertiliser around fruits and vegetables, mulch around fruit trees and bushes, and earth up potatoes.

• Start feeding all plants in pots and make sure that they don't dry out.

APRIL

• Look out for the first pests of the season. Organic or chemical controls can help you avoid the problems of slugs and snails attacking young seedlings, aphids – or blackfly – covering broad beans, and greenfly attacking the new shoots of plums and currants.

• Continue to sow seeds outside – April is often the best month to sow because the soil is getting warmer. Continue to sow seeds in the greenhouse.

• Plant potatoes.

• Plant up a herb pot for the patio.

• Keep weeds under control by hoeing around your fruit and vegetables.

• Under cover, sow fast-growing tender vegetables such as courgettes, French beans, marrows and runner beans.

MAY

• Continue to look out for pests. As well as slugs, snails and aphids, gooseberry sawfly is a common problem this month and you need to put codling moth traps in apple trees at the end of the month.

- In dry weather, water newly sown and planted crops.

- Plant out leeks, brassicas such as cabbage and calabrese, and celery and celeriac.

- Continue to sow salad crops and herbs regularly.

- Sow more French beans.

- Put the tender plants that are growing in the greenhouse outside to get them used to conditions before planting out at the end of the month (this is known as hardening off). If you don't do this, the change in conditions can 'shock' the plants and check their growth.

JUNE

- Plant out tender veg: either your own-grown plants, or just buy ready-grown ones.

- Protect strawberries from damage from slugs, from getting dirty with straw or mats, and from birds with netting or fleece.

- Keep weeds under control by hoeing.

- Keep removing the side shoots of tomatoes and feed them once a week. Make sure that you don't allow tomatoes in growing bags or pots to dry out.

- Stop cutting asparagus in the middle of the month. Mulch the rows with compost and give some fertiliser to build up the roots for next year.

- Thin out apples, plums and

pears if the branches are laden with small fruits.

JULY

• As soon as strawberries have finished cropping, cut back the foliage and remove any runners that grow from the mother plants.

• Cover blueberry bushes and other soft fruit with netting or fleece to protect them from birds.

• Cut down early peas and broad beans that have been harvested. Leave the roots in the soil to add nitrogen to it.

• Be prepared to spray potatoes against blight. Lift and harvest new potatoes.

• Continue to sow salad crops and weed among your crops.

• Prune blackcurrants as soon as the berries have been picked.

• Mulch around squashes and pumpkins with compost or manure and keep them watered well.

AUGUST

• August is the perfect time to sow Oriental crops such as pak choi and Chinese cabbage. Also sow spring cabbage and fennel.

• You should have lots to harvest this month – pick while young and fresh.

- Pull up any crops that have finished and sow fast-growing salads in their place, or if you're not using the ground for crops until winter or next spring, sow green manures.

- Sow overwintering onions and plant special new potatoes for Christmas.

- Summer prune apples and many other fruit bushes and trees.

SEPTEMBER

- Continue to sow Oriental vegetables, salads and herbs. Sow endive, land cress and lamb's lettuce for winter.

- Pinch out the tops of tomato plants to prevent fruits being formed that won't ripen.

- Pick sweetcorn and squashes as they mature.

- Start to harvest apples and pears as they reach ripeness.

- Dig up potatoes as soon as they finish flowering and if the foliage starts to yellow.

- Earth up or stake Brussels sprouts and other overwintering brassicas to help them stand up to winter gales.

OCTOBER

- Harvest all squashes before the first frost damages them. Finish lifting and storing potatoes.

- Dig over bare soil. Put all green plants and weeds in the compost heap.

- Plant garlic and broad beans.

- Cut back Jerusalem artichokes and pull up sweetcorn.

- Pick the last tomatoes from plants in the greenhouse.

- Clean out the greenhouse, and make the most of any under-cover growing space there (and in the porch and conservatory for winter herbs and salads.

NOVEMBER

- Order seed catalogues and fruit catalogues.

- Clear the soil of crops that are past their best.

- Pick up and pull off yellowing leaves from brassicas.

- Harvest leeks, celery, Jerusalem artichokes, parsnips and the last of the carrots and beet.

- Check the ties on trees and cover brassicas with netting to prevent bird damage.

DECEMBER

- Dig over any bare soil. Empty the compost heap and dig this into the soil.

- Prune grapes and do any winter pruning of fruit trees and bushes.

- Make sure that you add some garden items to your Christmas list!

GREENHOUSE INSECT MANAGEMENT

The warm, humid conditions and abundant food in a greenhouse provide an excellent, stable environment for pest development. Often, the natural enemies that serve to keep pests under control outside are not present in the greenhouse. For these reasons, pest situations often develop in this indoor environment more rapidly and with greater severity than outdoors. Pest problems can be chronic unless recognized and corrected.

Successful control of insect pests on greenhouse vegetables and ornamentals depends on several factors. Proper cultural practices can minimize the chance for initiation and buildup of infestations.Early detection and diagnosis are keys to greenhouse pest management, as well as the proper choice and application of pesticides when they are needed. The pests that attack plants produced under conventional greenhouse practices also infest plants produced in float systems. Float systems are especially prone to problems with fungus gnats, shore flies and bloodworms.

Some greenhouse insects can transmit diseases to the plants which are often more serious than the feeding injury that the insect causes. These insect "vectors" include some aphids, leafhoppers, thrips and whiteflies. In these instances, the diseases must be managed through early insect control.

COMMON GREENHOUSE INSECTS AND RELATED PESTS

Since greenhouse conditions allow rapid development of pest populations, early detection and diagnosis of pest insects are necessary to make control decisions before the problem gets out of hand and you suffer economic loss. Some common and important greenhouse pests to keep a close watch for are aphids, fungus gnats, thrips, whiteflies, caterpillars, leafminers, mealybugs, mites, slugs and snails.

Aphid cornicles

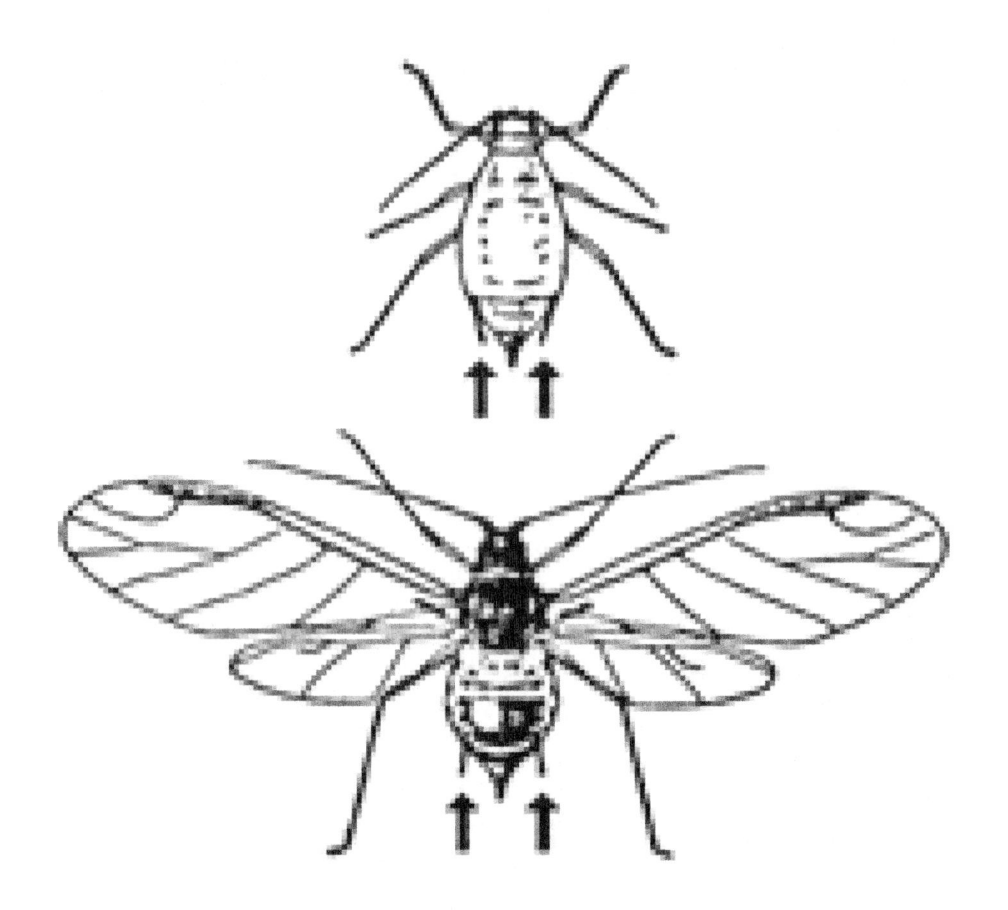

Aphids or plant lice are small, soft-bodied, sluggish insects that cluster in colonies on the leaves and stems of the host plants. They are sucking insects that insert their beaks into a leaf or stem to extract plant sap. They are usually found on and under the youngest leaves, and, in general, prefer to feed on tender, young growth.

Aphids are the only insects that have a pair of cornicles, or tubes that resemble exhaust pipes, on their abdomen.

Aphids multiply rapidly. In greenhouses, each one is a female capable of giving live birth to daughters in about seven days after its own birth. These asexually reproducing female aphids may be winged or wingless. Adult aphids can give birth to six to ten young per day over their 20- to 30-day life span. Enormous populations can build up in a relatively short period.

Feeding by aphids can cause leaves or stems to curl or pucker; this leaf distortion often protects the aphids from contact insecticides. Much of the sap they suck from the plant passes through their bodies and is dropped on the leaves as "honeydew." Ants, which feed on honeydew, are often found in association with aphid infestations. Black sooty mold often develops on leaves with honeydew.

Aphids can also transmit serious viral diseases. Managing these diseases usually requires control of the insect that transmits the disease. Aphid infestations usually begin with winged individuals entering the greenhouse through openings.

Insecticide applications to control aphids often must be repeated to manage infestations. Usually two to three applications spaced at three- to seven-day intervals, depending on the severity of an infestation, are necessary. Insecticide products need to be alternated for aphid control to delay development of resistance.

If you observe aphids that appear tan or off-color relative to the other aphids, they may be parasitized aphids known as "mummies." These naturally-occurring wasp parasites so important to aphid control are smaller than aphids. When these parasites emerge, they cut a round hole in the upper portion of the abdomen of the dead aphid and begin to search for their prey.

Fungus Gnats, Shore Flies and Bloodworms

The high humidity and moist organic growing media in greenhouses provide an excellent breeding area for several types of gnats. These insects are abundant outdoors where they can breed in virtually any accumulation of standing water that remains in place for several days. Adult and Larva

Fungus Gnats

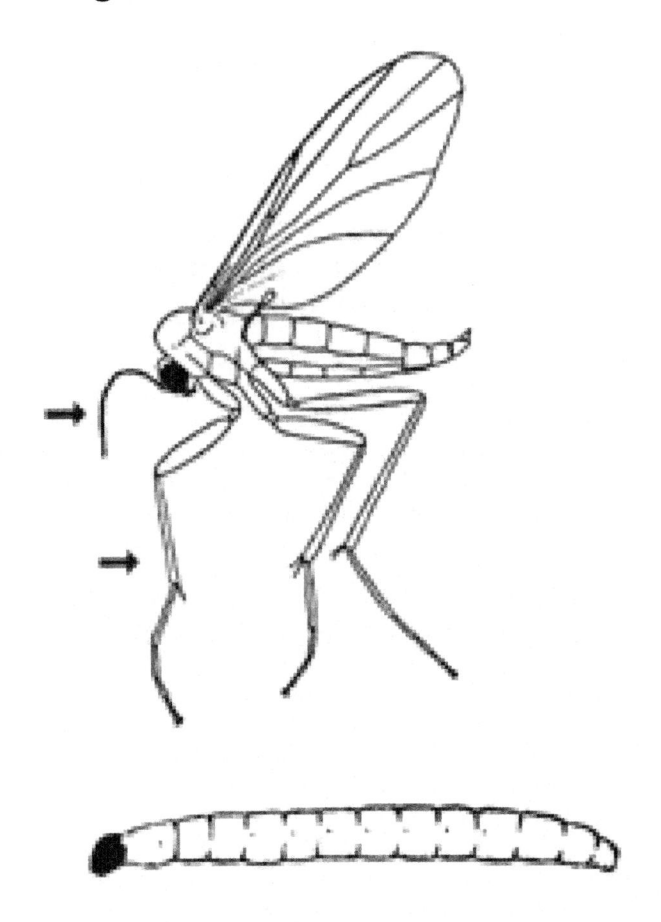

Fungus gnat larvae can be serious pests of some greenhouse plants. The larvae of most species are scavengers, feeding on decaying organic matter in the soil.

However, larvae of some species will feed on root hairs, enter the roots or even attack the crown or stem of the plant. Plants infested with fungus gnats generally lack vigor and may begin to wilt. Adults are frequently observed running on the foliage or medium before injury caused by the larvae becomes apparent.

Fungus gnats are small (1/8 inch) black flies with comparatively long legs and antennae, tiny heads and one pair of clear wings. Females lay tiny ribbons of yellowish-white eggs in growing media that hatch within four days. The clear larvae are legless and have black heads.

Larvae mature underground in about 14 days and pupate near the surface of the medium. They construct a pupal case made of soil debris. Adults live only about a week. Under greenhouse conditions, about 20-25 days are required to complete a generation. Larvae are somewhat gregarious and are found in clusters in the soil.

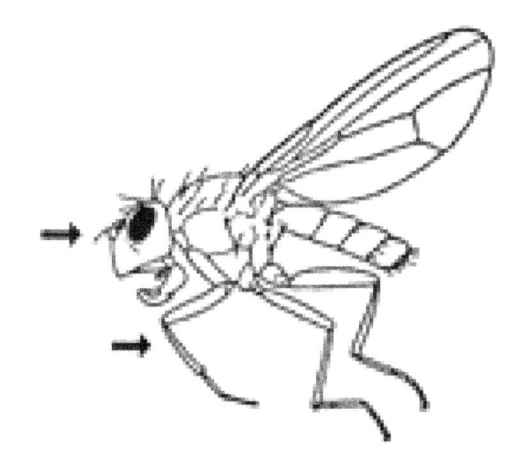

Shore Flies

Shore flies are gnat-like insects similar to fungus gnats. They differ in having short antennae, red eyes and heavier dark bodies. A pair of smoky wings with several clear spots can be seen when looking closely at the insect. They are good fliers and can be seen resting on almost any surface in the greenhouse. They resemble winged aphids, but aphids have two pairs of wings and the distinctive, tube-like cornicles on the abdomen.

Their life cycle is similar to that of the fungus gnat. The yellow to brown larvae, which may be up to 1/4-inch long, differ in having no apparent head. Both larvae and adults feed mostly on algae growing on media, floors, benches or pots. They rarely damage plant tissue, but the mobile adults may spread soil pathogens inside the greenhouse.

Bloodworms

Bloodworms are the striking red "worms" that may be seen wriggling in float plant water. These long, cylindrical larvae are similar to fungus gnat larvae in lacking legs and having a distinct brown head. The red is due to the presence of hemoglobin, the same oxygen-carrying material present in human blood. The presence of hemoglobin allows this insect to develop in water with a very low oxygen content.

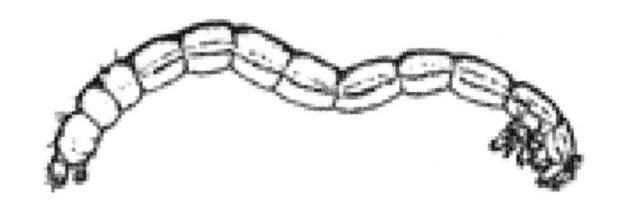

Bloodwarm

Bloodworms are common in stagnant water, animal watering troughs and other accumulations of standing water. These insects are close relatives of the mosquito, but the adults do not have sucking mouthparts and are not blood feeders. The larvae have chewing mouthparts and generally feed on algae or other organic matter in the water. They may be found in plant roots that grow through the bottoms of float trays but apparently do not cause significant injury.

While fungus gnats and shore flies live in "very wet" situations, bloodworms generally live entirely in water. Eliminating standing puddles around the area and keeping to a minimum the amount of exposed water surface in the float bed will reduce the presence of these insects.

Avoiding excessive watering to reduce moisture in growing media will help regulate these pests because they require high moisture. Highly organic soils and potting mixtures containing peat are attractive to egg-laying fungus gnats. Sprays or drenches containing Bacillius thuringiensis Serotype H-14 (Gnatrol) can be used to control fungus gnat larvae on ornamentals and nursery plantings in the greenhouse. This treatment is not effective against shore flies.

Thrips

Thrips are tiny, slender insects about 1/25-inch long. They range in color from light brown to black. They have four wings, each fringed with a row of long hairs, that are held flat over their back. Plant-feeding thrips cause economic damage when they infest the flowers, buds and young fruits of a crop.

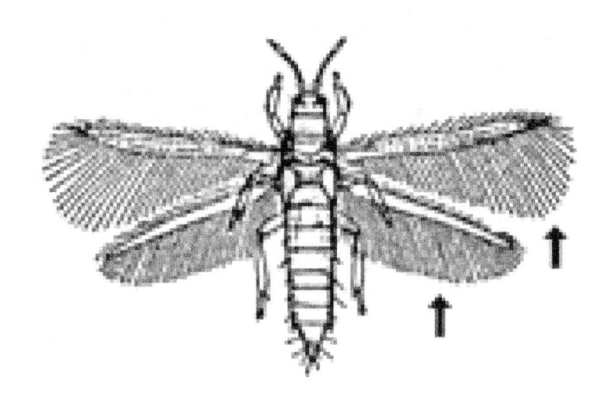

Thrips

Thrips feed by rasping the plant surface and sucking up the exuding sap. Heavily infested leaves have a mottled or silvery appearance. Female thrips insert eggs into slits in the leaf. Eggs hatch in two to seven days. Nymphs feed much like adults and molt four times during development. They are inactive during the last nymphal stage before becoming an adult.

Winged adults are carried into the greenhouse on contaminated plant material, or they fly in during the summer and continue to breed throughout the winter. Preventing infestations through the use of screens on ventilators, inspecting new material entering the greenhouse and controlling weeds in the greenhouse will help to manage thrips.

Several species occur in greenhouses. Thrips attack a wide range of plants in the greenhouse. Highly susceptible hosts include azalea, calla lily, croton, cyclamen, cucumber, fuchsia, ivy and rose. Various thrip species also transmit plant diseases. The most serious are the western flower thrips and onion thrips, which are vectors of tomato spotted wilt virus or impatiens necrotic spot virus. This virus attacks a wide variety of plants.

Greenhouse and Sweet Potato Whiteflies

Whiteflies are serious pests in the greenhouse and are often seen on fuchsias, poinsettias, cucumbers, lettuce and tomatoes. Through regular monitoring, these preferred hosts can be used as indicator "plants," alerting greenhouse managers to the first signs of whitefly infestations. These powdery white insects, about 1/12 inch in length, flutter from the undersides of leaves when the plants are disturbed. The lower surface of the leaves may be infested with all life stages of whiteflies.

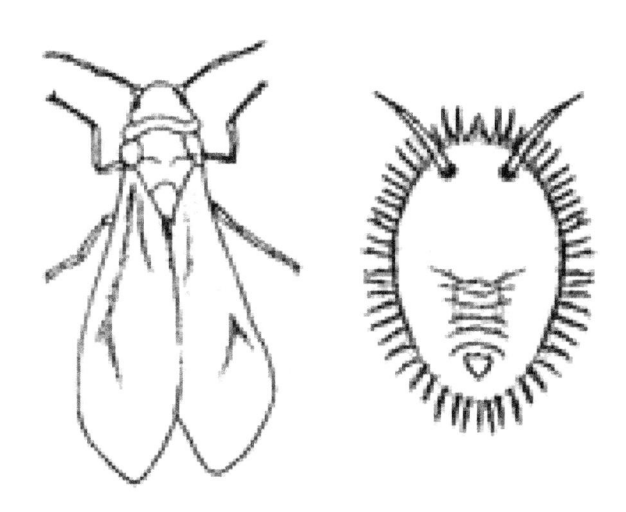

Whitefly and Larva

The female of these sap-sucking insects may lay 150 eggs at the rate of 25 per day. The newly emerged crawler moves only a short distance before settling down to feed. After three larval molts, the pupal stage is formed, from which the adult emerges. The entire life cycle takes 21-36 days, depending on the greenhouse environment.

The greenhouse and sweet potato whiteflies are similar in appearance but differ in their biology and control. Both whitefly species develop entirely on the undersides of leaves. Their life cycle may be as short as 20 to 25 days.

The sweet potato whitefly has a broader host range, higher reproductive potential, stronger resistance to insecticides and a powerfully phytotoxic enzyme system. This whitefly is a vector of gemini viruses in tomatoes. Control of these viruses relies on proper sanitation and control of the whitefly vectors.

Insecticides used to control adult whiteflies are usually ineffective against immatures. Because adult whiteflies often continue to emerge after these applications, insecticides used to control adults must be applied frequently, two to three times with three- to four-day intervals between sprays, to control infestations. Growth regulators used to control immature stages can be applied less frequently, at seven- to 14-day intervals as necessary, to control infestations.

A tiny parasitic wasp, Encarsia formosa, attacks the larval stage of whiteflies and sometimes occurs naturally in greenhouses. While they are not useful in controlling heavy whitefly infestations, they can be used successfully against early infestations under conditions that favor their development over the development of whiteflies (64°- 80°F).

After the parasitized larvae die and turn black, a parasite wasp will emerge and continue the beneficial process. Do not throw pruned leaves away without checking them for black larvae containing parasites. Leave these under plants for about one week until wasps have emerged.

This beneficial insect is very susceptible to insecticides. It is more effective in controlling greenhouse whitefly than sweet potato whitefly. It can be purchased commercially and introduced at intervals when whiteflies are first observed. See ENTFact-125, Vendors of Beneficial Organisms in North America, for more information.

Cutworms, Armyworms, Loopers and Other Caterpillars

All caterpillars are the immature stages of moths. They chew on leaves, stems and fruits of many kinds of plants. Infestations may begin when moths enter through ventilators or when infested plants are brought into the greenhouse. Cutworms can be serious pests of younger plants. They hide during the day in soil or mulch and feed on the plants at night.

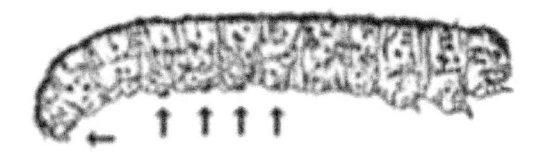

Cutworm larva (left) and Cabbage looper (right)
The cabbage looper can be a pest of greenhouse crops, especially lettuce. It can be distinguished by its pale green

color, three pairs of prolegs (small fleshy bumps on the underside of the abdomen) and looping movement (bringing the rear of its body up to the front legs before moving the front legs forward) similar to that of measuringworms. When monitoring for these insects, look for cut plants or leaves with large sections removed. Sprays containing Bacillius thuringiensis are effective against these pests.

Leafminer Fly and Larva

Leafminers

Leafminers are larvae of small flies. They damage plants by feeding between the upper and lower surface of the leaf. Damaged areas are light in color and narrow and winding. They increase in width as the larva grows. When fully grown, the larva may pupate in the leaf tissue or emerge from the leaf and fall to the gound to pupate. Each female fly will lay from 50 to 100 eggs by inserting them into pits made in the leaf surface. Because the damaging stages of the insects occur entirely inside the leaf, control with contact insecticides is ineffective once the damage appears. Infestations can be avoided through the use of good cultural practices, hand removal and disposal of infested leaves and use of chemical controls when necessary.

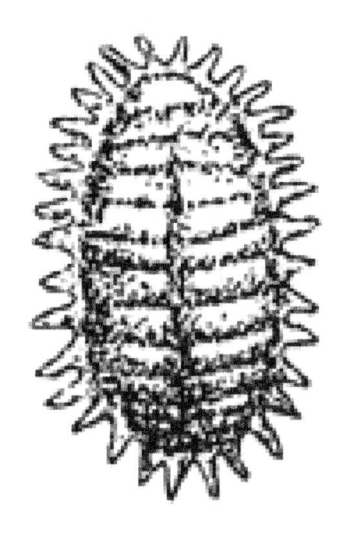

Mealybug

Mealybugs

Mealy bugs are small, soft-bodied insects which, like aphids, feed on plant sap. These insects are thickly covered with mealy or waxy secretions which provide some protection from contact insecticides. Some species lay eggs; others give birth to live young. Like aphids, mealybugs often produce large amounts of honeydew that results in sooty mold on leaves and other plant parts.

Mealybugs may infest almost any part of the plant. A wide variety of plants in the greenhouse are susceptible to mealybugs, but they are often seen first on crotons, hoyas and bamboo palms. Ants, which collect honeydew as food, are often seen in association with mealybug infestations.

Mites

Mites are sap-sucking pests which attack a wide range of greenhouse plants. Two species, the two-spotted spider mite and the cyclamen mite, can cause serious and persistent problems. These mites feed by piercing tissue with their mouthparts and sucking out cell contents.

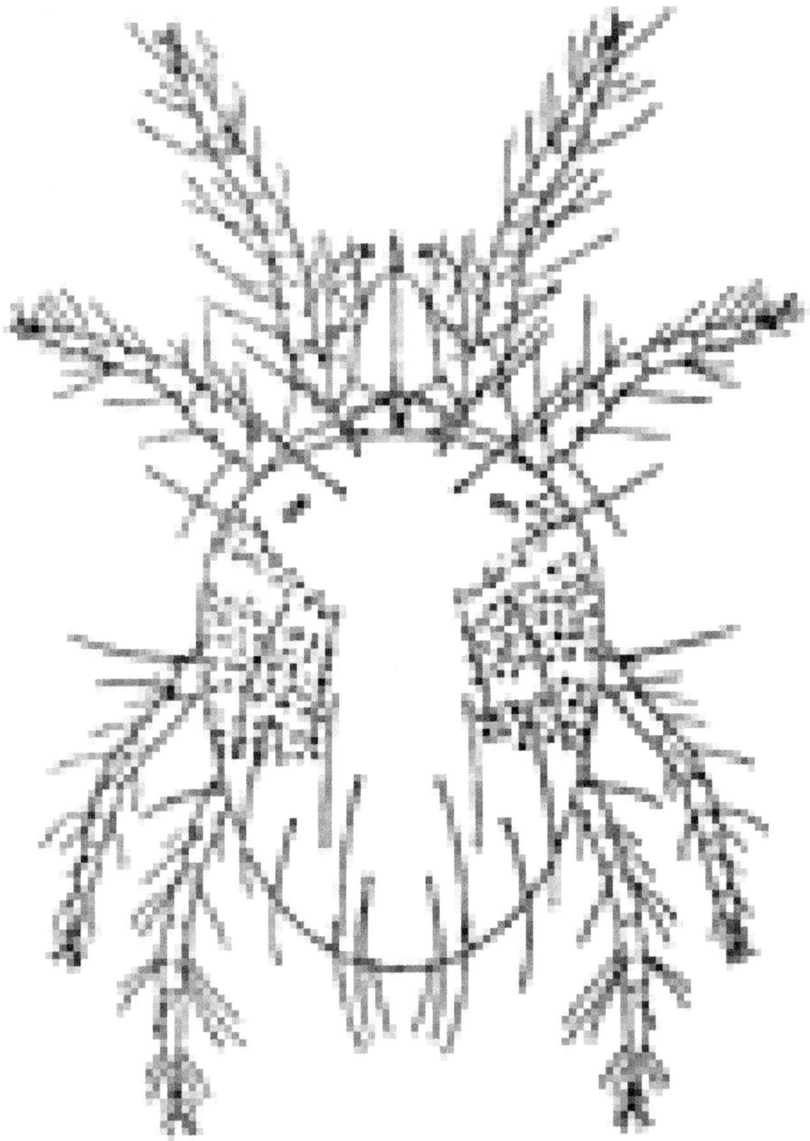

Two-spotted Spider Mite

Two-spotted spider mites are light to dark green with two distinctive black spots on the abdomen. Eggs are spherical and clear when first laid. After hatching, the larva has three pairs of legs, but later stages will have four pairs. Males are smaller with more pointed abdomens than females. Heavy infestations of the two-spotted spider mite produce fine webbing which may cover the entire plant.

Generally they feed on the undersides of leaves, giving the upper leaf surface a speckled or mottled appearance. Leaves of mite-infested plants may turn yellow and dry up, and plants may lose vigor and die when infestations are severe. Females can lay 200 eggs, and during hot, dry weather the life cycle may be completed in seven days. Marigolds, crotons, chrysanthemums, roses, impatiens, parlor palms, bamboo palms and ivy geraniums are highly susceptible to two-spotted spider mites and can be used as indicator plants to alert managers to infestations.

Cyclamen mites are minute, elliptical, semi-transparent, greenish mites. These mites thrive when the temperature is around 60°F and can complete their life cycle in about two weeks. African violets, cyclamen, dahlia, gloxinia and New Guinea impatiens are highly susceptible to cyclamen mites and can be used as indicator plants to alert greenhouse managers.

Depending on the type of plant attacked, cyclamen mites may infest the entire plant or be concentrated around the buds. Infested leaves become distorted and often curl inward; foliage may become darker than that of healthy leaves. Because of their small size, infestations often go undetected until the damage is severe. Usually it is the nature of the injury, not the mites themselves, that alerts greenhouse managers to cyclamen mite infestations.

Mites can easily be moved to infested plants on clothing, so always examine infested benches and other hot spots last during greenhouse inspections. Often, it is better to discard infested plants than to attempt to control the problem with pesticides. If control is attempted, isolate the infested plants to reduce potential spread.

Resistance to pesticides has increased the difficulty of controlling these pests. Because mites primarily occur on the undersides of leaves, applications of contact miticides should be directed at both the lower and upper leaf surfaces. Mite eggs are resistant to some insecticides, so repeated applications are often necessary to control infestations. Two to three applications spaced five days apart may be necessary. Miticides with different modes of action need to be alternated, so different products are used to control each subsequent mite generation.

Several species of mite predators are commercially available. These are usually released when mites first appear and should be evenly dispersed throughout the greenhouse. If mite infestations are heavy, consider spraying with an insecticidal soap before releasing predator mites. Selection of the proper predatory mite species will depend on greenhouse temperatures and humidity. If predatory mites are used, early release at the first sign of mite infestation is critical. Unlike a miticide, predatory mites will take some time to control infestations. See ENTFact-125, Vendors of Beneficial Organisms in North America, for a list of predatory mites and suppliers.

Slugs and Snails

Two-spotted spider mites are light to dark green with two distinctive black spots on the abdomen. Eggs are spherical and clear when first laid. After hatching, the larva has three pairs of legs, but later stages will have four pairs. Males are smaller with more pointed abdomens than females. Heavy infestations of the two-spotted spider mite produce fine webbing which may cover the entire plant.

Generally they feed on the undersides of leaves, giving the upper leaf surface a speckled or mottled appearance. Leaves of mite-infested plants may turn yellow and dry up, and plants may lose vigor and die when infestations are severe. Females can lay 200 eggs, and during hot, dry weather the life cycle may be completed in seven days. Marigolds, crotons, chrysanthemums, roses, impatiens, parlor palms, bamboo palms and ivy geraniums are highly susceptible to two-spotted spider mites and can be used as indicator plants to alert managers to infestations.

Cyclamen mites are minute, elliptical, semi-transparent, greenish mites. These mites thrive when the temperature is around 60°F and can complete their life cycle in about two weeks. African violets, cyclamen, dahlia, gloxinia and New Guinea impatiens are highly susceptible to cyclamen mites and can be used as indicator plants to alert greenhouse managers.

Depending on the type of plant attacked, cyclamen mites may infest the entire plant or be concentrated around the buds. Infested leaves become distorted and often curl inward; foliage may become darker than that of healthy leaves. Because of their small size, infestations often go undetected until the damage is severe. Usually it is the nature of the injury, not the mites themselves, that alerts greenhouse managers to cyclamen mite infestations.

Mites can easily be moved to infested plants on clothing, so always examine infested benches and other hot spots last during greenhouse inspections. Often, it is better to discard infested plants than to attempt to control the problem with pesticides. If control is attempted, isolate the infested plants to reduce potential spread.

Resistance to pesticides has increased the difficulty of controlling these pests. Because mites primarily occur on the undersides of leaves, applications of contact miticides should be directed at both the lower and upper leaf surfaces. Mite eggs are resistant to some insecticides, so repeated applications are often necessary to control infestations. Two to three applications spaced five days apart may be necessary. Miticides with different modes of action need to be alternated, so different products are used to control each subsequent mite generation.

Several species of mite predators are commercially available. These are usually released when mites first appear and should be evenly dispersed throughout the greenhouse. If mite infestations are heavy, consider spraying with an insecticidal soap before releasing predator mites. Selection of the proper predatory mite species will depend on greenhouse temperatures and humidity. If predatory mites are used, early release at the first sign of mite infestation is critical. Unlike a miticide, predatory mites will take some time to control infestations. See ENTFact-125, Vendors of Beneficial Organisms in North America, for a list of predatory mites and suppliers.

GENERAL STRATEGIES FOR INSECT AND MITE MANAGEMENT
Cultural Controls are Essential

Pests are generally brought into the greenhouse on new plant material. Others may enter the greenhouse in the summer when the ventilators are open. Many are able to survive short periods of time between harvest or plant removal and production of the next crop. Cultural controls are the primary defense against insect infestations.

The following cultural practices will help to prevent pest infestations:

1. Inspect new plants thoroughly to prevent the accidental introduction of pests into the greenhouse.

2. Keep doors, screens and ventilators in good repair.

3. Use clean or sterile soils or ground media. Clean or sterilize tools, flats and other equipment.

4. Maintain a clean, closely mowed area around the greenhouse to reduce invasion by pests that develop in weeds outdoors.

5. Eliminate pools of standing water on floors. Algal and moss growth in these areas can be sources of fungus gnat and shore fly problems.

6. Dispose of trash, boards and old plant debris in the area.

7. Remove all plants and any plant debris, clean the greenhouse thoroughly after each production cycle.

8. If possible, allow the greenhouse to freeze in winter to eliminate tender insects like whiteflies.

9. Avoid overwatering and promote good ventilation to minimize wet areas conducive to fly breeding.

10. Avoid wearing yellow clothing which is attractive to many insect pests.

11. Maintain a weed-free greenhouse at all times.

12. Eliminate infestations by discarding or removing heavily infested plants.

Monitoring

Early detection and diagnosis of pest infestations will allow you to make pest control decisions before the problem gets out of hand. It is good practice to make weekly inspections of plants in all sections of the greenhouse. When monitoring, select plants so that they represent the different species in the greenhouse. Pay particular attention to plants near ventilators, doors and fans. At least 1% of the plants need to be examined on each monitoring visit in the greenhouse.

Insect monitoring devices should be used in the greenhouse. Yellow sticky cards (PT Insect Monitoring & Trapping System, Whitmire, St. Louis, MO) are highly attractive to winged aphids, leafminer adults, whiteflies, leafhoppers, thrips (blue cards can also be used with thrips), various flies and other insects. White sticky cards can be used to detect fungus gnat adults. These can be used to alert you to the presence of a pest and identify hot spots in the greenhouse. One to three cards per 1000 square feet in the greenhouse is recommended. Cards should be changed weekly.

Typically, these sticky cards are suspended vertically just above the tops of the plants. They can be attached to sticks or hung on string. If you cannot identify a trapped insect, contact your county Extension agent for assistance.

Mass trapping products such as sticky tapes are also available for management of thrips, whiteflies, leafminers and fungus gnats. While sticky cards are primarily used just to alert you to insect infestations, mass trapping tools are used to reduce and manage insect infestations. Mass trapping relies on using enough surface area of the attractive sticky tapes to capture and reduce pest numbers. Care should be taken to keep monitoring and trapping products dry and free of debris. This will maintain effectiveness of the traps.

Biological Control Agents

Natural enemies are commercially available for control of some greenhouse pests. For a listing of sources, see ENT-53, Vendors of Beneficial Organisms in North America.

Levels of pest control obtained with beneficial organisms will vary greatly depending on a number of factors, including:

• species of pest involved

• species of natural enemy used

• timing of release of natural enemy relative to pest buildup and crop development

• numbers of beneficials released

• greenhouse temperature and range of fluctuation

- time of year

- condition of the beneficials at release

- pesticide usage before and after release of beneficials.

Biological control generally requires more time than pesticides to bring a pest population under control. Natural enemies require time to disperse from release sites and to search for prey or hosts. Appropriate natural enemies should be released as soon as the pest is detected in the greenhouse.

Natural enemies do not provide sufficiently rapid control of pests that are already causing serious losses, and they will not generally eradicate an infestation. In some instances, using an insecticidal soap or other non-residual insecticide is recommended to reduce the infestation before releasing the natural enemies. Knowledge of pest biology and monitoring of pest populations are critical to determining when to make releases.

Greenhouse managers should avoid unnecessary insecticide/miticide applications before and after release of natural enemies. If insecticide/miticide treatments are required, limit treatments to pest "hot spots" to avoid treating the entire greenhouse. Use a selective, short residual pesticide if possible. For example, Bacillius thuringiensis (Bt) products can be used to control caterpillars without harm to natural enemies in the greenhouse.

Beneficial Organisms Commercially Available for Greenhouse Pest Management	
Beneficial organism	Pest controlled
Parasitic wasps, Encarsia formosa	Whiteflies
Parasitic wasps, Aphytis melinus	Scales
Leafminer parasite, Dacnusca sibirlica and Diglyphus isaea	Serpentine leafminers, ungus gnats
Predatory mites, Amblyseius californicus, Phytoseiulus longipes and Phytoseiulus persimilis	Spider mites
Predatory mites, Amblyseius cucumeris and Amblyseius mckenziei	Thrips
Lady beetles, Hippodamia convergens and Cryptolaemus montrouzeri	Various soft-bodied insects and eggs
Green lacewings, Chrysoperla carnea	Various soft-bodied insects and eggs

Pesticide Management

Greenhouse operators need to maximize the effectiveness of insecticides and miticides. To provide adequate control, a pesticide must beapplied at theproper rate, when thepest is present. Coverageand sufficient pressureare needed to penetrate dense foliage and reach the target pest. This is especially important for sucking insects that infest the lower surface of leaves. Older, lower leaves can be removed to open the canopy of some crops to increase spray coverage. Insecticide or miticide applications must sometimes be repeated frequently to maintain a pest at acceptable levels.

Timing of pesticide applications is important. Some pests are vulnerable to pesticides only at certain stages in their life cycle. For whitefly management, begin control measures early. If control action is delayed until an abundance of adult whiteflies can be seen, then numerous eggs and immature stages, which are more difficult to control, are usually present.

With a limited number of pesticides available for greenhouse use, it is always a concern that pests may develop resistance to pesticides. Managers should rotate among different pesticides for successive applications when controlling specific pests. Rotations must include pesticides belonging to different chemical classes that use different modes of action to control the pests. This will prevent, or at least delay, the development of resistance to a particular pesticide.

To aid pesticide applications, plants that are frequently infested by thesame pest and can be legally sprayed with the same material should be grouped together. This will reduce the potential for misapplications to unlabelled crops. Additionally, moving infested material through the greenhouse can spread an infestation to other areas.

WHY CLEAN YOUR GREENHOUSE?

A routine or annual greenhouse cleaning is essential to prevent unwanted pests and diseases from moving in. While this protected environment nurtures plants, it also provides the perfect conditions for pests to thrive or overwinter. Insects and mites will hibernate in cracks and crevices, plant pathogens will continue to exist in the soil, algae will grow in the lines, and gnats will reproduce on organic residues.

These are risks to any plants you are hoping to foster come springtime, and success requires a combination of removing crops, disinfecting, preparing, and sanitizing. While this maintenance should take place regularly for year-round greenhouses, a fall clean up at your season's end is enough for the seasonal greenhouse.

Stop Overwintering Pests and Diseases

Some pests and diseases are more likely to overwinter in a greenhouse. Thankfully you can usually predict what they'll be by paying attention to the type of crops you are growing.

Cleaning Your Greenhouse Step-By-Step

Plants

Choose a time when the weather is favorable for a few days and empty the greenhouse of all plant matter, including any weeds that are trying to get a foothold on earthen floors.

Take note of any existing diseases or pests and dispose into a compost away from susceptible plants.

Inspect any citrus or tropical plants for developing colonies of scale, mealy bug, whitefly, or spider mite. Use safe management technique sand quarantine until the problem fully resolves. For more information, read our article about Spider Mites: How to Identify and Control Them Naturally.

Pots and Accessories

Wash all greenhouse accessories including pots, trays, and equipment thoroughly with soapy water and let sit in a oxygen bleach solution of 3/4 cup oxygen bleach to one gallon of water.

Recycle or dispose of disposable seed trays and pots, moving them far from the vicinity of the greenhouse as soon as possible.

Soils

Old soils can contain pathogens like pythium, fusarium, rhizoctonia, fungus gnats, grubs, root aphids, and more. Remove soils from pots and beds and let compost for a year or more to rejuvenate.

Replace with clean, disease-free soil purchased at a reputable supplier in the spring or just prior to planting new crop. This includes the soil in your pots and beds as well as the soil between paths and under benches.

Rake or sweep out any debris and treat the entire exposed area with diatomaceous earth at the very end of the clean up procedure when your greenhouse will sit dormant.

Irrigation

Disinfect irrigation and holding tanks. Irrigation lines and holding tanks develop algae and can host thousands of gnats, which are a threat to small roots. Using 3/4 cup oxygen bleach to one gallon of hot water, flush lines, soak any dripper heads, and scrub out holding tanks or fertilizer reservoir.

Structure and Wood

The greenhouse structure provides great refuge for overwintering pests. Metal frame greenhousesaren't as susceptible but still need disinfectant. Wood is the worst for providing the right cracks and crevices that spider mites, thrips, aphids, and whitefly all use as a hideout.

Wash your entire greenhouse structure and glass down using an oxygen bleach solution.

Apply a vegetable-based horticultural oil onto all exposed wood. This is best done using a brush to ensure the oil reaches into any cracks to suffocate hiding pests.

Let the greenhouse sit empty and dormant over the winter or for as long as possible. Ensure clean soil is used to replace previous soils and only introduce pest and disease free plants.

Ongoing Greenhouse Cleaning and Maintenance

Throughout the growing season, avoid overlapping planting or intercropping to reduce transferring problems from one crop to another.

Deal with "green bridges" or weeds and volunteer plants that can act as hosts for problems between crops as quickly as possible.

Remove plants that develop diseases or harbour pests from the growing area as soon as they are noticed. This will not only limit the spread, but also make clean up easier.

Avoid recontamination. Disease and pests can be transferred from one place to the next on shoes, clothing, and new plants.

Practise good hygiene and do not visit the greenhouse after visiting areas of potential threat.

Always wash pots to be reused and disinfect your tools on a regular basis. The more effort you put in the less risk you will hav

CONCLUSION

Today, entire crops and fields utilize greenhouse technologies to produce more food with higher crop yields. ... Food growers can reduce or eliminate the use of harmful pesticides, which is essential for organic farming. Greenhouses protect plants from adverse weather events such as hail, snow, and intense heat.

Modern greenhouses can be a viable solution for creating habitats for out of season crops. Even though there are high upfront expenses associated with greenhouse technology, with successful management, it's possible to see increased revenue from your crops. Prices for produce fluctuate as vegetables come in and out of season. Out of season crops can fetch larger profits on the market, especially when grown locally. Produce sold at farmer's markets is often the best way for consumers to get high-quality fruitsand vegetables. Buying out of season vegetables like lettuces and strawberries, for example, is easier with greenhouse technology. Whether saving money on monthly grocery bills or increasing revenue, gardeners and farmers who build greenhouses will find it an excellent investment when managed successfully. On a wider scale, the trends in greenhouse growing will surely influence the ways in which we ship, distribute, and purchase raw produce in the future.

Printed in Great Britain
by Amazon